UNIVERSITY OF
WOLVERHAMPTON

Drama
in
Primary
English
Teaching

Suzi Clipson-Boyles

David Fulton Publishers
London

David Fulton Publishers Ltd
Ormond House, 26–27 Boswell Street, London WC1N 3JD

First published in Great Britain by David Fulton Publishers 1998

Note: The right of Suzi Clipson-Boyles to be identified as the author of this work has been asserted by her in accordance with the Copyright, Designs and Patents Act 1988

British Library Cataloguing in Publication Data
A catalogue record for this book is available from the British Library

ISBN 1–85346–540–2

Typeset by FSH Print and Production Ltd, London
Printed in Great Britain by Bell & Bain Ltd, Glasgow

Contents

Preface

This book has been written especially for:

- trainee primary teachers/new primary teachers
- experienced primary teachers who feel unsure about teaching drama
- language coordinators who need to help their staff to develop a drama framework
- headteachers who wish to encourage their staff to include more drama in their teaching.

The main aim of the book is to introduce all the components which need to be considered in order to plan, assess and teach drama as part of the National Curriculum requirements for English. This comprehensive and integrated approach is known as *New Wave Drama*. The approach is a newly-emerging mode of working, as it combines the best pedagogies from more traditional experiential child drama approaches with more recent views on the inclusion of theatre arts in primary education.

The components you need in order to teach drama have been separated out into individual chapters to enable you to examine specific aspects in more depth, and to assist easy reference. However, it is important to remember that in reality these components are inextricably linked.

An integrated approach to English, where oracy, reading and writing are part of a complex linguistic inter-relationship, is at the heart of all good practice when teaching language. Likewise, there should be a healthy symbiosis between assessment and planning. Drama as an art form can take a discrete place in the curriculum, and yet even when that happens there is inevitable overlap between content and skills from other areas, in particular English. That is the nature of primary education at its best. In order to make explicit this integration, examples of drama activities are provided throughout and there is useful cross referencing between chapters.

For those who are new to teaching drama, it is advisable to introduce activities into your practice gradually – in bite size chunks! The book emphasises throughout that there are many approaches to drama, and different time-scales from five minutes upwards, depending on the purpose of the activity. Start with something which feels comfortable to you, where you will feel firmly in control and which has clear learning objectives. The results will almost certainly inspire you to try more!

Many thanks to all the student teachers and teachers whose energy, enthusiasm and creativity during drama courses at Oxford Brookes University have reinforced my belief that drama is a powerful pedagogy. Thanks to all the children I have taught over the years whose ideas and responses have reinforced my belief that drama is a wonderful art form through which they can explore, express and expand their learning. Thanks also to Laura and Claire for allowing me to reproduce their writing; and to Andy, Ben and Charlie, whose patience, understanding and tolerance have enabled me to produce this book!

Extracts from *Drama in Schools* (1992) have been reproduced with the kind permission of The Arts Council of England. Material from the National Curriculum is Crown copyright and is reproduced by permission of the Controller of Her Majesty's Stationery Office. The material on pages 66–68 was originally published in *Reading On! Developing Reading at Key Stage 2*, eds. D. Reid and D. Bentley (© Scholastic Ltd. 1996) and is produced here by kind permission of Scholastic Ltd.

Suzi Clipson-Boyles, Oxford, July 1998

Chapter 1

Introduction to Drama

The most successful work in primary schools...shows that drama not only has value as a vehicle for work in other subjects; it is also important in its own right and is widely appealing to primary children.

(HMI 1990: p 5, para. 3)

In this introductory chapter you can read about:

- what is meant by 'drama'
- the changing emphasis on drama in primary education
- the value of drama in the learning development of primary children
- the different roles of drama in the primary curriculum.

Why teach drama?

Choosing to incorporate drama into your ongoing classroom practice means that you will be equipping yourself with a powerful and efficient teaching approach. You will be providing your pupils with experiences which will motivate them and help them to learn effectively through direct and purposeful interactive language activity. You will also be offering them alternative and creative means of expressing their ideas and presenting the outcomes of their learning, which will exrend their creative awareness.

However, drama is sometimes regarded with trepidation by teachers who have had little or no experience of teaching it, and OFSTED inspections are identifying that drama is not being taught adequately in many primary schools. To try and redress the balance, this book has been written with four main aims in mind:

- to support teachers in learning about how to use drama approaches in their work
- to make explicit all the valuable language learning which can take place during drama activities
- to demonstrate how the National Curriculum requirements for drama in English can be delivered
- to illustrate the vast learning potential which drama has to offer, as an arts subject and as a pedagogy.

What is drama?

Finding a useful definition for drama has often been difficult because views have been polarised by different theoretical debates. On the one hand, there are those who believe that drama is a pure art form, directly aligned with creative expression, theatre and performance. The purists in this camp dislike the notion of drama being used as a 'vehicle' for teaching other subjects, seeing such an approach as a dilution of the art form and an erosion of its status. At the other extreme, there are those who regard drama as a process of self exploration and development – a means by which children can interact (rather than act) during simulated or improvised experiences provided to assist their learning. The purists in this camp dislike any notion of theatricality, rehearsal or performance.

As with most extreme beliefs, there is also a middle ground. This is not, however, a watering down of both views at the halfway point, but rather a relationship between the two, within which there are many different forms of drama to be used. These all have different but equally valuable contributions to make to good quality primary education, from experimental writing in the role play area through to the sophisticated presentation of extracts from Shakespeare. This is now widely agreed to be a useful, balanced and educationally-appropriate model for use in primary schools, by those who fully understand the learning needs of young children, and the practicalities of fulfilling those needs for a class of 35 as part of a packed curriculum!

In order to help you understand how this rich and varied model of drama has developed, let us first look at the emergence of drama in the primary school during the last 60 years.

The background to primary drama

The 1944 Education Act was filled with a post-war determination to provide children with a new kind of education which would develop them in a balanced and holistic way. Freedom and self expression were clearly of critical importance to a nation that was recovering from the repression of war, and the arts were to play an important role in this revolutionary approach, in ways which had never been seen before.

The work of Peter Slade (1958) was instrumental in developing drama away from the traditional 'performance of plays' approach and towards child development and experiential methods. These offered children the opportunity to play with ideas and experience situations as a means of gaining insight into and understanding of different themes. It can be no coincidence that this was taking place during the same decade as the work of theorists such as Piaget (1952) whose research was highlighting the links between interaction, speech, thought and learning development.

Brian Way (1967) was another key figure who continued to develop this approach in the 1960s, and this momentum led to the legendary work of Dorothy Heathcote (Wagner 1979) and Gavin Bolton (1979) during the next decade when drama played a significant part in the primary curriculum. Their work demonstrated astounding results with children; in-depth learning, the development of understanding, effective organisation of ideas and confident expression of those ideas. This work went from strength to strength, into the early 1980s. However, concerns were starting to emerge about the curriculum, and the suspicion that there were serious gaps in children's learning, particularly in literacy and numeracy, was addressed in the 1988 Education Act. This had a major impact upon the arts in general, and drama in particular.

Since the Act, the place of drama in primary education has undergone major changes and challenges. During the early stages of the introduction of the National Curriculum from 1989 onwards, drama changed from being a rich and thriving part of primary education, into a disappearing rare breed. This was due partly to curriculum overload (teachers were having to deal with vast quantities of new subject matter in all areas), and partly to the fact that drama was not included in the National Curriculum as a discrete subject. It was, however, mentioned in the Orders for maths, history, geography, science and English as a useful teaching approach to certain aspects of learning in those subjects.

It is easy to see, in retrospect, that there was concern about this in certain quarters. In 1990, HMI produced a report on the teaching and learning of drama in the primary school which endorsed the educational value of drama both as an arts subject and as a teaching method. In 1991, the National

Curriculum Council produced a poster entitled *Drama in the National Curriculum*, offering guidance to teachers on how they could use drama to teach across the curriculum. The Arts Council of Great Britain responded to the omission of drama as a foundation subject by producing its own programmes of study (see Appendix 3) and end of key stage statements for drama as part of the report *Drama in Schools* (1992). This very useful document highlighted the place of drama as an arts subject and emphasised the entitlement of all pupils to the experiences and knowledge of this important aspect of our culture. Whilst unequivocally representing the place of drama as an arts subject, the report nevertheless acknowledged the important part drama has to play in other aspects of children's learning. 'Drama can contribute powerfully to the quality of learning in many areas of the primary school curriculum.' (p.1, para. 1.4.)

Despite these belated, and somewhat reactive, attempts to persuade teachers to include drama in their planning, the tide of curriculum content had swept over the land of pedagogy, and drama was almost totally reduced to the obligatory Christmas performances (whose robustness to survive are a clear indicator of the tremendous importance they have for parents and pupils).

Today, as the government acknowledges that the curriculum is too overloaded with content, policy is turning, once again, to pedagogy. The National Literacy Strategy Teaching Framework (1998) offers guidance to teachers, not only on the detailed requirements of a comprehensive literacy programme, but also on how to teach that programme. At the same time, the statutory 'slimming down' of the foundation subjects which aims to provide teachers with the opportunity to make more appropriate choices about the selection of content, means that there will be more time and flexibility to incorporate drama back into primary teaching. A return to the key issues of how children learn will inevitably highlight the relevance of drama as a pedagogy, so let us now consider why that is the case.

Why should drama be included in the primary curriculum?

There should be no doubt that drama has a crucial part to play in the primary curriculum. Four major reasons for this are:

- it is an art form central to our cultural heritage
- it is a means of contextualising and activating language
- it assists the learning process through active engagement
- it is a valid medium for expressing and communicating ideas.

Let us examine each of those in more detail.

Drama as an art form

Drama is a universal cultural phenomenon, crossing geographical boundaries as it emerges in many forms around the world. Likewise, it goes back through history – the word 'drama' is derived from the Ancient Greek (meaning 'action') – and the literature and approaches to theatre through the ages are well-documented. Although *theatre* appears in many styles, even within cultures, the drama is the unifying element which is at the heart of them all. The power of story, the transmission of knowledge, the shaping of ideas and emotions into an art form which is alive, dynamic and interactive, all make connections with human response which resonates with life itself! So how can we ignore this vital aspect of human behaviour? It is part of our heritage, it is part of communication, and all children should have equal opportunities to enjoy it, learn about it, use it, and be enriched by it. This will only happen if it is embedded within our educational system.

Drama and language

Language is at the core of that system, as indeed it is at the core of human communication itself. Literacy and oracy are high priority areas in the National Curriculum. They also support children's learning in other subjects because the curriculum, particularly at Key Stage 2, is designed with the assumption that children can read, write, listen to instruction and talk about their work. Drama puts language into action in ways with which children can identify, respond and learn. It brings language alive by providing meaningful contexts. These include roles, purposes, and audiences, all of which give the language authenticity in the eyes of the children.

Drama and learning

Drama assists the learning process by enabling children to engage actively with their subject matter. In the home corner, children play out the roles of adults and encounter situations from new perspectives. Their responses to that can reshape their thinking because the process of active engagement and externalisation of thought are contributing to the ways in which things become organised in their minds. Older children taking part in the simulation of a Viking funeral will be applying their existing knowledge to the situation, acquiring new knowledge and theories from the actions of others, and developing new thoughts and responses in ways which would never arise from simply listening to an account. There is much evidence to support the hypothesis that all these things will also be retained more efficiently in the long-term memory because of the interactive nature of the learning process.

Drama as a means of expression

Children produce work in a variety of formats in school: topic books, writing for displays, fiction, reports, newspapers, paintings and so on. Drama offers yet another medium for the expression and presentation of learning. There are different ways this can happen, as you will see as you continue to read this book. It might be a group of five children displaying freeze frame pictures of Aztec scenes after researching this from non fiction; it might be a puppet play performance of Macbeth, or it could be an in-role presentation of why a new motorway should or should not be built. As with any piece of work, these products should be created with high expectations of children's preparation, organisation and communication. Standards should be high, and the assessment of learning should be paramount. Records of such work can easily be made in this age of video, and writing activities might also be linked to the drama, as you will discover in Chapter 8.

Where does drama belong in the primary curriculum?

The many different approaches to teaching drama described in this book are like a box of tools which are used for all sorts of tasks within primary education. Theatre education is just one of those tasks. From five-minute interviews in pairs to celebratory performances in assembly, there is a wide range of places where drama can usefully fit. The polarised views on the functions of drama are of no help to busy teachers. Not only do they create conflict when trying to share out precious time, they also exclude opportunities for learning by narrowing down the potential of drama tools into tight and prescriptive headings.

The reality is that an integrated approach to curriculum delivery, for example teaching referencing skills during geography work, is time effective, and enhances the learning by making conceptual connections between skills and across areas of knowledge. However, an integrated approach should not exclude the necessity for making explicit to the children the specialist values of certain skills and knowledge such as the powerful effects of theatricality. In other words, it is quite feasible to plan a comprehensive arts approach using subject matter which is also helping children to learn about other things.

Having established the strengths of integration, it is nevertheless useful to separate out features of the potential of drama in order to understand better where there might be useful areas of overlap. Figure 1.1 identifies three major roles of drama, both as a teaching tool and as a discrete arts subject. It lists examples of how drama can be used to develop language skills, explore and build concepts and knowledge in other curriculum areas, and be employed in performance, again incorporating other National Curriculum subjects. The term 'Theatre Studies' has been used to distinguish where drama might appear in the curriculum in its own right. The more general use of the term 'drama' in the column headings has been used to describe the use of drama as a teaching and learning method.

DRAMA FOR LANGUAGE LEARNING	DRAMA FOR ACQUIRING CONCEPTS AND KNOWLEDGE	DRAMA FOR PERFORMANCE
English: oracy e.g. using language in role	Art e.g. exploring feelings and moods (after drama)	Music e.g. creating effects to communicate ideas
English: reading e.g. interpreting scripts	Design and Technology e.g. human machine inventions	Physical Education (Dance) e.g. character narratives
English: writing e.g. home corner writing	Geography e.g. in-role discussion of environmental issues	
	History e.g. Victorian children at work (simulation)	
	Maths e.g. weighing – shop role-play area	
	Science e.g. water cycle dance-drama	
Theatre Studies e.g. analysis of screenplay	Theatre Studies e.g. Greek Theatre (history)	Theatre Studies e.g. character portrayal in Christmas play
	R.E. e.g. exploration of relationship issues	
	Cross Curricular Issues e.g. marketing new products (Industry)	

Figure 1.1 The roles of drama in the primary curriculum

It is easy to see that there could be much overlapping between the columns of the table. For example, oracy skills would be developed during the debate in geography, the exploration of Greek Theatre could sit appropriately within a topic on Ancient Greece, and the Christmas play might provide good opportunities for reading for meaning and the use of appropriate expression. Nevertheless, it is useful to be aware of the discrete frameworks if you are to build a sound professional understanding of the workings of drama. This matrix is a simple overview to help you to start thinking about the different ways in which drama can be used. A more detailed analysis of such connections is discussed in Chapter 10.

It is both desirable and feasible to provide a comprehensive drama programme throughout all primary schools – desirable because of the richness of the learning opportunities, and feasible because of the universal and flexible nature of drama described in this chapter. However, the statutory requirements for drama are embedded within the National Curriculum Order for English, and this is where we must start if we are to feel confident that we are fulfilling those requirements. The next chapter describes the relationship between drama and English, and how the prescribed remit can be achieved.

Chapter 2

Drama and English

Where it is done well, the teaching of drama has a strong influence upon the development of language and literacy, and the children's self confidence.

(HMI 1990: p.7, para. 3)

In this chapter you can read about:

- the statutory requirements for drama
- the part which drama has to play in language learning
- the place of Theatre Studies in the curriculum for English
- the planning implications for primary teachers.

The statutory requirements for teaching drama

It is a requirement of the National Curriculum that primary children experience and participate in drama activities as part of their education at Key Stages 1 and 2. This is set out in the Order for English where it appears *explicitly* in various places. Figure 2.1 identifies 16 different reference points in the Programmes of Study.

Drama is also *implicit* within many other parts of the requirements for English. The potential for teaching language skills through drama activities is so great that it is not possible to list all the possibilities here. However, Figure 2.2 provides some examples.

EXTRACT	REFERENCE
• talk for a range of purposes…including imaginative play and drama	KS1 AT1 Para.1a
• participate in drama activities, improvisations and performances of varying kinds	KS1 AT1 Para.1d
• respond to drama they have watched as well as that in which they have participated	KS1 AT1 Para.1d
• exploration and discussion of word games	KS1 AT1 Para.3b
• read plays (on their own and with others)	KS1 AT2 Para.1a
• read complete short texts including playscripts	KS1 AT2 Para.2c
• prepare, present and act out stories and poems	KS1 AT2 Para.2c
• enacting stories and poems	KS2 AT1 Para.1a
• presenting to audiences, live or on tape	KS2 AT1 Para.1a
• participate in a wide range of drama activities, including improvisation, role-play and the writing and performance of scripted drama	KS2 AT1 Para.1d
• in responding to drama…evaluate their own and others' contributions	KS2 AT1 Para.1d
• re-present features of…a radio or television programme	KS2 AT1 Para.2b
• activities that focus on…language used in drama, role-play and word games	KS2 AT1 Para.3b
• independent reading of play scripts, by groups and the whole class	KS2 AT2 Para.1a
• write in response to…plays	KS2 AT3 Para.1b
• use the characteristic forms of…drama scripts	KS2 AT3 Para.1c

Figure 2.1 Requirements for drama in the Order for English: explicit references

EXTRACT AND SUGGESTED MODE OF DRAMA	REFERENCE
• talk for a range of purposes *(role-play)*	KS1 AT1 Para.1a
• describing events, observations and experiences *(improvisation)*	KS1 AT1 Para.1a
• structure their talk in ways that are coherent and understandable *(performance)*	KS1 AT1 Para.2a
• extensive experience of children's literature *(hot seating characters)*	KS1 AT2 Para.1a
• read with fluency, accuracy, understanding *(reading and performing play scripts)*	KS1 AT2 Para.2a
• write in a range of forms *(writing in home corner)*	KS1 AT3 Para.1c
• communicate to different audiences *(simulated meetings)*	KS2 AT1 Para.1b
• express themselves confidently and clearly *(presenting work outcomes in role)*	KS2 AT1 Para.2a
• consider in detail the quality and depth of what they read *(improvising inter-textual hypotheses)*	KS2 AT2 Para.2b
• write for varied purposes *(writer in role)*	KS2 AT3 Para.1a
• distinguish degrees of formality in writing for unfamiliar audiences *(audiences provided through role-play)*	KS2 AT3 Para.2a

Figure 2.2 Requirements for drama in the Order for English: examples of implicit references

We can see quite clearly from these two lists that there is an interconnectedness between the English and the drama as each supports the other in ways which can enrich learning and support understanding. It is also interesting to note that the explicit references are weighted more heavily towards plays, performance and theatricality than the implicit examples, which tend to rely more heavily on the experiential language learning to be offered by drama. In other words, the statutory requirements place drama towards the 'theatre end' of the continuum described in Chapter 1.

Despite this, the fact that drama does not appear as a foundation subject in its own right has offended some, who believe that the subordinate place of drama within English reduces its status and ignores the importance of arts education. To debate the politics and philosophy of such issues is not the main aim of this book. Instead, it is designed to offer, within the existing statutory framework, a positive and creative approach to teaching drama which:

- supports and extends language and literacy learning
- enhances language and learning in other subject areas and
- offers children the opportunity, where apppropriate, to learn about, participate in and develop a critical awareness of drama as an art form.

Communication is the central component of all these three, and therefore it would seem appropriate to help teachers to develop their planning for drama in ways which are integral to their planning for language.

Language and learning

Language is central to human activity and behaviour. It is all around us as speech and text, and it is within us as thought and interpretation. It is taking place continuously and interactively in billions of transactions per second and consequently it radiates from the centre of any situation we care to choose.

Imagine a busy supermarket. There is print everywhere, giving information, instruction, persuasion, explanation and even warning. And think of all the people talking! Different ages and in different roles – explaining, complaining, questioning, answering, counting, instructing, and so on. The supermarket is an absolute buzzing hive of language!

It is small wonder, then, that English is a core subject in the National Curriculum. It is at the heart of learning and at the heart of life itself. The best quality teaching of language and literacy skills is that which is embedded within contexts that reflect the interactive and dynamic nature of language as described above. Learning activities which enable children to learn about language by using language are not just desirable because the children enjoy them (although that has a major impact on motivation which in turn helps the learning process), but are essential because they reflect the true nature of language and enable children to participate as active learners, rather than vegetate as passive receivers! Drama enables you to provide such interactive contexts through which children can learn about language, and improve their user skills.

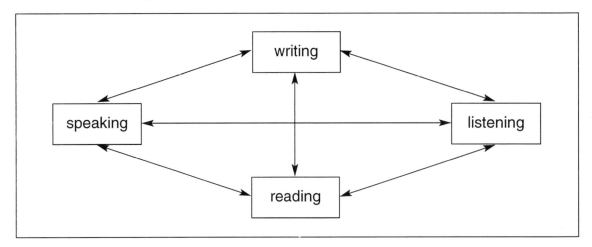

Figure 2.3 The integration of language skills

The model in Figure 2.3 illustrates the components of language required to be taught by the Order – speaking, listening, reading and writing. They each sit in a separate box, representing the fact that it is possible to focus on each in isolation, e.g. handwriting exercises. However, the model also includes arrows between them to highlight the relationships which should be considered when planning activities, e.g. discussing ideas, planning, writing and reading a book for the class library. An integrated approach to language is the most effective way for children to learn. The Programmes of Study for both key stages endorse this belief, each beginning the statement that: 'Pupils' abilities should be developed within an integrated programme of speaking, listening, reading and writing.' (DFE, 1995, pp.4 & 11)

Drama adds a powerful dimension to language work because it enables the children to become active and interactive users. The model in Figure 2.4 attempts to illustrate this. The language skills appear, this time in a three-dimensional box, still connected by their arrows, but no longer separated into discrete units. The drama activities, represented in a second box below, generate eight processes:

- exploration
- research
- empathy and awareness
- planning
- organising
- repeating
- consolidating
- communicating.

These are all processes (and you will probably think of more to add to the list) which can arise out of the drama, and which set in motion the use of language skills. For instance, an improvisation of conversations between the animals in Anthony Browne's *Zoo* (1992) would aim to generate particular types of talk (e.g. description of feeling, debate about zoos) and could lead to follow-up poetry describing the animals' feelings. The processes can also feed back into the drama (note the two-way arrows), for instance the children might go on to read *Gorilla* by the same author (1983) and discuss the similarities in features, author style etc. The drama will have particularly helped the

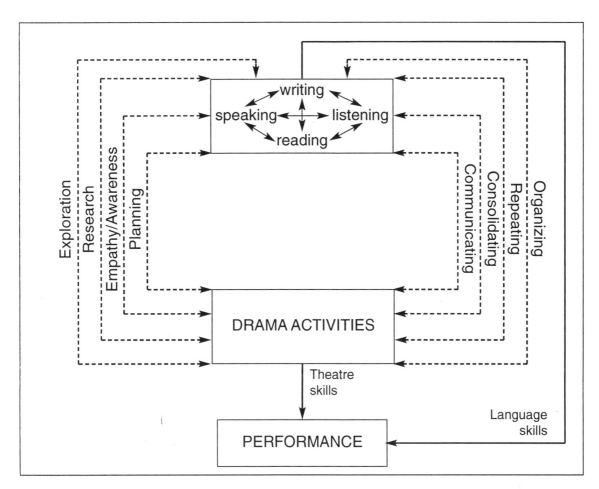

Figure 2.4 The impact of drama upon language activities: a wrap-around model

children to develop:

- an empathy with the characters
- an awareness of the deeper meanings in the books; and
- the ability to express the emotions in ways which a simple discussion might not have produced.

There are two further points to make about this wrap-around model. Firstly, the four language components, reading, writing, speaking and listening, are overarching labels for vast numbers of language skills. Imagine the complexity of a model which might attempt to illustrate this; the number of variables operating between all those skills and the eight processes would be countless! That is a wonderful toolbox from which to select when planning your English teaching…

Secondly, you will have noticed the box containing Performance in the bottom right-hand corner, positioned here because it does not always have to be central to the drama. As you continue to read this book, you will learn that performance is not an obligatory outcome of drama, although children need to be given some opportunities to work in this mode. Sometimes it will be appropriate to communicate their drama in other ways, such as a discussion about how they felt about a simulation once it is over. The communication process arrow represents this in the model.

Theatricality: to be or not to be?

Should primary school children be learning about theatre? That is the question! The traditional educational drama approaches of the 60s stressed that drama was not about acting, but about experiencing. However, as drama starts to re-emerge in primary education it is taking on a new more integrated shape – this has been called New Wave Drama (Clipson-Boyles 1997). New Wave Drama incorporates all the rich and valuable learning to be offered by experiential drama, but it also makes space for the theatricality which is part of the art form of drama. 'Once we move beyond the notion that all learning in drama is best acquired through engagement in unrepeated improvisations, students must learn to shape their symbolic dramatic representations to create more effective metaphors of their emerging understandings.' (Somers 1994)

'Sharing' work with others is a common feature of primary education. Performance is a mode of sharing, but one which requires particular skills and knowledge of drama as an art form-theatricality. If children have been developing a critical awareness through regular visits to (or from) professionals throughout the primary years, their own work is going to be inspired and enriched. Alongside this, teachers need to feel confident about providing opportunities for children to explore the creation and construction of theatrical drama. Chapter 5 offers basic guidance on this aspect.

Implications for planning

When starting to incorporate drama into your planning for English, you will need to keep two questions firmly in your mind. Firstly, how can drama be developed as a discrete subject which enables you to cover the explicit requirements within the English Order and to develop children's awareness and use of drama as an art form? Secondly, how can you use drama to provide purposeful language learning opportunities across the curriculum? This might mean that you 'teach drama' once or twice a week within the first category, whilst also 'using drama as a resource' several times during the week across a range of subject areas.

Having said that, there will always be overlap, as described in Chapter 1. For instance, Key Stage 1 children could create a puppet performance about 'life when grandma was a girl'. Inspired by a professional performance, they are learning much about the powers of communication in theatre, and yet they are also learning about history. Likewise in Key Stage 2, you might be using your discrete drama session to explore the theatrical presentation of a point of tension in a reworking of *The Iron Woman* (Hughes 1993), but there is also valuable learning taking place about characterisation and literature, as described in the Programme of Study for reading. Chapter 11 will help you to understand how you can make the most of integration, by presenting a model of planning.

Chapter 3

Different Drama Methods

Drama is an interactive, living art form which reflects a variety of styles, genres and approaches...There are as many ways of teaching drama as there are teachers teaching...

(Geoff Readman and Gordon Lamont 1994)

In this chapter you can read about:

- why you need a range of drama approaches
- the different purposes for using drama
- a description of each of the main tools commonly used for teaching drama
- a practical example of each tool in use.

The need for a range of drama tools

The term 'tools' has been selected quite intentionally for use here as it provides a good analogy of the teacher as carpenter. Just as carpentry requires different tools for certain tasks, so does the teacher need to employ a range of teaching approaches to facilitate different types of learning experiences for the pupils. Teachers are well aware of this choice when planning other subjects, but when considering drama they can sometimes be misled by the belief that there is only one kind of drama lesson. The notion of drama being a noisy, unstructured and chaotic activity involving the whole class in the hall is likely to put many teachers off wanting to include drama in their planning, and who could blame them! Other people worry that drama is about training children to be wonderful actors, and feel that they lack the expertise to conduct such a specialist task.

There is no such thing as 'the typical drama lesson'. Instead, there is a huge range of approaches to drama, all of which have different learning processes to offer. It is also important to remember that drama is not just a whole-class activity which always needs a large space and a long stretch of time. As in other subjects, you can vary the group size, the location and the length of time spent on the activity, and these elements of planning and organisation are discussed in detail in Chapter 4.

Identifying the purpose of the drama

There can be many reasons for including drama in your planning. The wider issues relating to this have already been discussed in Chapter 1, and how these purposes are connected to teaching English were the subject of Chapter 2. In this chapter, as the range of drama tools is described, it is important to consider how they should be selected, and this should always be done by asking, 'What is the purpose?'. Good planning always includes a moment to think what the children will experience through the planned activity. How will it seem from their point of view? Will it provide the necessary focus, information, time and opportunities for them to learn, practise or consolidate the intended skills and understanding?

The different drama approaches described in this chapter offer a range of experiences which can suit different purposes. It is not appropriate to list all possible purposes as these could be potentially endless – and, of course, each method can be used for more than one purpose. However, the following examples are intended to illustrate how drama can be used for sound pedagogical reasons in order to meet a particular teaching and learning need.

- mime   to assist memory through recap by miming and guessing
- tableaux   to provide a form for the presentation of research
- dynamic duos   to practise particular forms of speech
- script reading   to practise reading with expression
- home corner   to encourage experimental writing
- dance drama   to provide an art form for the expression of feelings on a theme

Description of the modes

The modes have been divided into four categories. This categorisation is not intended to impose boundaries or limitations. Indeed, there are areas of overlap between them, for example children will develop their work in role sometimes, towards creating a piece for performance. They have been organised in this way to try and assist your understanding of the broad potential. The four categories are:

1 Working in role
2 Working with sound
3 Stylised drama approaches
4 Working towards performance.

Working in role

Working in role means, as suggested by the name, taking the role of a character, real or imagined, in order to explore and develop an understanding of the character's experience within a given situation. The experience in question might be about responses to events, dealing with relationships, making decisions and so on. The function of role-play is not to 'act out' the part so that an audience can be convinced by the role, but rather to experience the role from within:to pretend to be a character in order to behave, think, speak and feel as the character would behave, think, speak and feel. This enables the children to learn from within a context, through a primary learning experience. There are different ways of working in role, and each of these can be employed for various purposes.

Role-play areas

The home corner is a familiar sight in many nurseries and KS1 classrooms. Dressing-up clothes, home implements and child-size furniture provide a setting for young children to play out the roles of adults, and in doing so help to develop their spoken language skills and social skills along with many other concepts, from pouring liquids to using telephone directories. Home corners can be transformed into other themed areas, usually to link with a particular aspect of work in the curriculum, e.g. shops, cafe, fire station, post office, dentist's surgery, space station and so on. The quality of the learning which takes place through such play depends very much on the quality of the provision. For example, placing special 'props' which relate to a story which you have just read to the class will encourage the children to play the characters from the story, extend and adapt the storyline and so on. Children need to know that their time is restricted in the role-play area, that their teacher values the play which is happening in there, and that they are accountable for their actions.

Dynamic duos

This approach is where the children are in role in pairs. It is a useful way of working because it can take place in the classroom for short periods of time. It can be used for many purposes, in particular the use of more formal language for a specific situation and to provide material for follow-up writing. It is usually very tightly structured, with the teacher giving clear briefings beforehand, clear signals to begin (e.g. a countdown from five), an agreement that no-one comes out of role until it is time, and a clear signal to indicate when that should happen (e.g. the shake of a tambourine). In other words, it is not an open-ended meandering, but a focused and specific piece of work where the teacher is observing and has high expectations.

EXAMPLE
Making a telephone enquiry
Time: 3 minutes

After a whole-class discussion about wildlife parks, ask the children to consider how they would need to speak on the telephone to make an enquiry about the animals if they were making a special TV programme. What questions would they need to ask and how would they ask them? How should the person who works at the park answer such enquiries? Should they, as part of their job, speak in particular ways? Sitting back-to-back, Child A rings Child B to find out certain details from a local wildlife park. After two minutes, get them to change roles. Giving feedback on 'good practice' might precede a repeat of the conversation in which they try to improve their first attempt.

 EXAMPLE
Reasoned argument
Time: 5 minutes

After a whole-class introduction on the issues of green-fields development, the children take on the roles of: a) the politician who wants to provide more housing; and b) the headteacher of a country village school who is concerned about the diminishing sites in his/her area. The role play is of a radio discussion where each has to express their views and debate the issues. The importance of turn-taking, making points clearly and giving reasons for disagreeing with the views of others should all be discussed before going into role. This might be followed up with one pair volunteering to replay their efforts for the whole class who would then be invited to comment on what was effective and why.

Hot seating

For this approach, the only person or people in role are those in 'the hot seat'. The hot seat is the place where a person sits to be questioned by pupils. It can take place as a whole-class activity, or in smaller numbers with various hot seated characters around the room being questioned by smaller groups of pupils. The person in the hot seat could be the teacher in role, a child in role, a group of children in role, or a visitor in role. The role played might be a character from fiction, a historical character, a famous person, or an imaginary person, depending on why this approach has been selected. It is an excellent way of getting children to ask searching questions either to seek information, use information or explore inferred meaning. It provides an opportunity to frame questions, listen to the questions of others, hear replies and extend thinking beyond the known.

Exploration beyond the text

Time: 10 minutes

After reading a story to the whole class, explain that you are going to pretend to be the main character – it is a good idea to have a prop relating to the story to assist with this. Choose a child to take over as teacher. They will introduce you and invite children with their hands up to ask questions. Make it clear to the children when you are in and out of role, e.g. by changing seats or removing the prop etc. Once you return to being yourself, give feedback on the questions they asked and discuss the fact that so much more happens in stories than just the bits we read!

 EXAMPLE

Victorian child labour

Time: 10 minutes preparation/10 minutes hot seating

Provide the children with information (books/worksheets/pictures) on Victorian Child Labour. Explain that they have ten minutes in which to become 'experts' and that four children will be selected to go into the hot seat for questioning by the rest of the class. They will be in role as Victorian children. At this stage, do not tell them whom! After ten minutes, gather the whole class together, having placed four chairs at the front. Select four children and put them by the door while you explain that these time travellers have kindly come along to answer questions. Explain that you will be listening to the questions carefully to see how much they have learned. After the hot seating, give feedback on how the questions were asked and answered, and ask the children to comment on what they have learned.

Writer in role

Putting the children into role in order to write can not only provide more purposeful contexts for the writing, it can also be tremendously motivating by adding an element of fun and pretence. Clearly, this concept can be applied in various ways ranging from writing telephone messages in the role-play area to composing a group letter-in-a-bottle from a whole class who are marooned on a tropical island! This tool will be discussed more extensively in Chapter 7, but the following examples show how using drama can really help to bring the writing alive.

 EXAMPLE

Planning a teddy bears' picnic

Time: 10 minutes whole class discussion/10 minutes writing

Now that Goldilocks has made friends with the three bears, they have decided to plan a grand picnic party for all the teddies in the area. In groups of four, each child taking one of the four roles, ask the children to make a list. These could be differentiated according to ability groups, for instance one group might be making a list of foods, whereas another group might be writing the timetable or invitations for the picnic.

EXAMPLE ___TV script writing___

Time: 20 minutes preparation/20 minutes writing/20 minutes feedback

Explain that many soap operas are written by teams of script writers. Show the last ten minutes of a favourite series such as 'Neighbours' or 'Byker Grove'. Hold a whole-class discussion, with you in role as the series editor, to brainstorm ideas about the next episode, including such issues as plot development and character motivation. Divide the children into script writing teams of three and allow 20 minutes for writing. Pair up each team with another team, and in turn ask each team to read the script aloud. The other team then gives feedback on the script in role as the editing directors.

Reader in role

Reading in role can be used to help children develop concepts of the many functions of reading. It can also provide a particularly helpful framework for reluctant readers who perhaps lack confidence in more formal reading situations. Use of this mode can range from children pretending to read a newspaper in the home corner to a 'news-reader' reading a script for the camera. The full extent of reading in role is discussed in Chapter 6.

 EXAMPLE

___Reading the Register___

Time: 5 minutes

Young children usually love pretending to be teacher! Provide a laminated list of names with a sheet for ticking attached. As the child calls out the names and ticks, you can mark the official version!

 EXAMPLE ___Science radio programme___

Time: 40 minutes preparation/10 minutes showing time

The children work in groups of four or five for this task, preferably each group on a different day of the week in order to space out the showing times. Together they research a particular aspect of a science topic which is part of the current classroom work (e.g. Electricity Now and Then). This should include reports on experiments, background knowledge from text books and mock interviews as appropriate. They prepare a radio programme to perform to the rest of the class. For this they will need to write a clear script which they will read from behind a screen. (This could, of course be recorded, but the discipline of having to read loudly, clearly and accurately from behind the screen, in role as reporters and interviewees usually helps to maintain the focus and improves the fluency and expression of the reading.) NB It is important to play them a short extract from a radio programme first in order to model the approach – introduction of topic, what will be in the programme today, reporting, presentation of different views and so on.

Guided action

Guided action is usually a whole-class activity. The teacher talks through a series of imagined events into which the children enter and participate. The teacher is not in role for this, but maintains control through the external narration of events. Guided action allows you to structure the activity tightly where you are describing actions and imaginings in great detail. However, it can also offer opportunities for more open-ended work which is stimulated by the preliminary instructions. For example, you may have talked the children through a walk across fields, over stiles, over stepping stones across a river. You will have described trees, hedgerows, animals, the warm sun on their faces and the cool grass against their feet. Then you might ask them, in groups of four, to find a suitable spot for a picnic, and to start unpacking all the things they have brought with them. In this way, you have established the mode of working, provided lots of starting points to assist their imaginings, and set up a framework for them to develop their own ideas on from there. Guided action can be used in many different ways, ranging from a short five-minute experience as an introduction to a discussion, to a longer exploration which eventually leads into a whole-class spontaneous improvisation with you in role.

 EXAMPLE

Use of geographical terms (hill, river, stream, track, road etc.)

Time: 5 minutes guided action/5 minutes teacher in role

You will need a large space such as the hall. Explain to the children that they are going to follow the journey which Goldilocks took when she discovered the house of the three bears. Each child should find a space so that they can work independently. Talk them through walking down the path of Goldilocks's house, opening and closing the gate, off down the track, the birds singing, coming to the main road, crossing carefully to the other side, into the forest and so on. As you describe this journey, you will be able to use terminology which you have introduced as part of your geography
work, for example, over a hill, round a farm, through a wood, across a river or stream. Once they have reached the three bears' house, tell them that they now have to find their way back with a partner, this time without your help. Before they start out, discuss all the features of the journey to remind them, getting as many of the answers from them as possible. When they are safely back at Goldilocks' house they should sit in the garden and have an imaginary glass of juice and a piece of cake while they are waiting for everyone else to settle! Praise those who do this well. This activity could be used as a preliminary stimulus to map drawing.

 EXAMPLE

A Voyage with Francis Drake

Time: 10 minutes preparation/10 minutes guided action

Show the children pictures of Elizabethan ships and discuss the conditions on board. Describe the sorts of provisions which needed to be stored on board, and the length of time they were at sea. In the hall, ask the children to lie on their backs and close their eyes. Describe their journey back through time (taped music can help to set the atmosphere). Then describe the scene of a port. When they open their eyes they are there and need to get to work. Talk them through a range of activities one at a time, such as rolling barrels of water up the gang planks, driving sheep on board into pens, carrying sacks of flour and so on. All the time, your voice is acting as narrator to their movements. Make it as dramatic as you can! Move on to pulling in the gang planks, hauling up the anchor, untying ropes on the dock side and raising the sails. As the ship sails off into the dark night, those on watch take up their posts, but your children have to take their sleep. They make their way down the ladders into the bowels of the ship and climb into their hammocks, tightly packed, side by side, and eventually silence falls. The music, or any other pre-agreed signal, brings them slowly back to the present. This could be used as a starting point for writing such as poetry about the feelings of those leaving home, or a captain's log. Alternatively, you may allow the children to continue the imagining as a spontaneous improvisation in groups of four, in order to develop a story of something which happens on board.

Guided imagery

This is very similar to guided action, but the children remain seated, or lie on the floor, with their eyes closed and imagine what you describe. This is usually used as a preliminary to discussion or improvisation. Your voice narrates, asking the children to imagine…Sometimes you should leave spaces for them to fill in pictures or ideas of their own. It is important to speak quite slowly, and not too loud when using this method.

 EXAMPLE

Journey down a rabbit hole

Time: 3 minutes guided imagery/5 minutes discussion

'Now that you have your eyes closed, try to picture a lovely green field. It has long grass, dandelions, tall trees around the edges, waving gently in the breeze… Suddenly, you see a little brown rabbit sitting up and looking round. He starts to run towards the trees. You are following him quietly, and you see him disappear into a hole between the roots of a huge tree. As you stare at the tree, you realise that the tree is getting bigger, and bigger, and bigger. No! It's you who are becoming smaller and smaller and smaller and smaller. The rabbit hole now looks like a huge cave, dark, a long tunnel stretching out before you. How do you feel? (PAUSE) Now you are starting to walk slowly into the tunnel…'

 EXAMPLE

The tip

Time: 5 minutes guided imagery/10 minutes discussion

Take them on a journey to a tip, but include lots of pauses for them to think up their own responses, e.g. 'As you stare at the piles and piles of rubbish, what do you see?' *or* 'Something starts to emerge from the rubbish slowly. What do you see?' This could be used as a stimulus to creating freeze frames making statements about the environment.

Spontaneous group improvisation

This approach can be used for small groups or the whole class. It can take place after a short instruction from the teacher, or as a follow-on after guided action or imagery. The children go into role and make up the action spontaneously, allowing the story to develop in ways which are unplanned. It is important to establish certain ground rules when using this approach.

(a) Have a clear signal to indicate when they are in role and not in role so that you can maintain control quickly and effectively (see Chapter 4).

(b) Explain that coming out of role during the improvisation spoils the illusion for the others in the group.
So, even when things go wrong, they should solve the problem as the characters, rather than reverting to self!

(c) Encourage the children to build on each other's ideas rather than ignoring them. In other words, one person's 'discovery' can become a shared experience for the group.

 EXAMPLE

Using language appropriate to a role or situation

Time: 5 minutes introduction/10 minutes improvisations

In this example you might be discussing with the children how you should talk to a shop

---

assistant when you are taking something back for a refund. First discuss the situation, then ask the children about how we should speak in this situation. Choose two children to improvise for the rest of the class. Repeat three times with different pairs of children, then let them all have a try back at their tables. Give a count-down so they know when to start pretending, and use a pre-arranged signal to call a halt. Give feedback.

(KS2) EXAMPLE   *Exploring themes from a text*

Time: 10 minutes introduction/5 minutes improvisation/10 minutes discussion.

Select a suitable chapter from your current class story which ends with a range of options open to the main character. Discuss the structure of chapter endings and the author's purpose in leaving it at a point of tension. Ask the children for their predictions about what might happen in the following chapter. Ask for volunteers to improvise a possible event from the next 'scene'. Show several options and discuss the implications of each in terms of the whole story development. Discuss the characters as portrayed in the improvisations. Were they behaving appropriately? How do authors maintain characters' responses?

Reconstructed improvisation

This approach is a development of the previous one. It enables the children to go back over their initial improvisation and shape it into a practised piece either to show to others or to use as a basis for writing scripts or stories. The initial spontaneous improvisation serves the purpose of getting the ideas to flow, and this reconstruction process provides the opportunity to select and shape those ideas for an end product. This involves moving into a more theatrical mode, where the children are making informed decisions about how they create and communicate work for performance to others.

(KS1) EXAMPLE   *Assembly on kindness to others (RE)*

Time: 10 minutes reconstruction

After spontaneous improvisations of playground scenes, discuss with the children how bad incidents can be 'put right', and who are the real superstars in such situations. Reconstruct the bad incident and the person putting it right (e.g. saying sorry, sharing a snack, asking someone to join in the game etc.). Replay the children's ideas, using their own words, but also asking them if they need to change any of it to show in assembly. Repeat to practise and put into a running order. It would also be a good idea if the children can freeze into 'statues' after they have had their turn. The final format would be, run on, play the scene, freeze, next group run on, play their scene, freeze, etc. You might like to ask them what message they could all say together at the end. Young children can come up with some wonderful ideas of their own!

(KS2) EXAMPLE   *Victorian family entertainment*

Time: 20 minutes

In groups of four or five, the children should use information books to find out how the Victorians entertained themselves in the evenings without television. It would be important, of course, to discuss the distinctions between rich, middle class and poor families. Allow them to choose roles to play and improvise scenes to demonstrate their findings. They should then evaluate these and reconstruct them into a smooth-running format, possibly with a narrator.

Simulation

A simulation involves improvisation but is less spontaneous because it involves elements of planning and preparation which lead to known outcomes. The children might or might not be involved in that planning and preparation. Simulation is a useful process to use when you wish to be in role yourself. Before starting, the teacher explains to the children exactly what is going to happen. This may involve the children in setting up the room in a particular way. Other preparations may include research from information books, character planning, the gathering of costumes or props and so on. The children will know what is going to happen before the commencement of the simulation. The value of this approach is that it provides opportunities for certain types of experiences where children can speak, listen and observe within a situation to which they might not normally have access.

 EXAMPLE   ***A Christian wedding***

Time: 10 minutes preparation/10 minutes simulation

Discuss love, marriage and weddings from different religions, and ask for information from the children about the weddings they have attended. What similarities are there between weddings from different religions? Describe the main features of a Christian wedding, then ask the children how the room should be set to create a church. Arrange the chairs accordingly, with a table for the altar, flowers, bible, etc. Decide who is going to be who – bride, groom, parents, bridesmaids, relations, vicar, choir etc. It is probably a good idea for you to take the role of vicar so that you are in a position to maintain control. Insist that once they are in the church area they must keep pretending to be the person they have chosen. Allow them to arrive gradually. A tape of organ music could help to set the atmosphere if you can obtain one. Edit the service appropriately so that it doesn't last too long! Singing one verse of each hymn will help here! After the event, discuss issues arising, such as the significance of festivals, religion and love, promises, emotions, listening supportively etc. It would also be important to use terminology throughout this session which does not make assumptions about all children. For example, 'Some people choose to get married...' 'Some couples who get married decide to get married in a church...' and so on.

(KS2) EXAMPLE   ***Protest meeting about a proposed multi-storey car park***

Time: 10 minutes preparation/20 minutes simulation

In the context of study on the influence of local developments on human activities, tell the children that a multi-storey car-park is to be built in the centre of a rather small country town. Show them a map on a large flip chart or OHP with key features of the town, roads, and the site of the new car-park. To make it really controversial you could even decide that it will be built on the site of a playing field!

Divide the children into groups of three, and give them a card with information such as: 'You are from the town council. You want this to go ahead because it will bring more trade to the town.' 'You are parents of local school-children. You are worried that the planned site will mean more traffic along the road where your children walk to school.' Allow the children five minutes to plan their arguments, and also to build up character profiles about themselves: age, job, personality, views etc. Discuss with the children how the room would be arranged for a public meeting in the Town Hall, and move chairs and tables accordingly. Ensure that there is an effective chairperson, and brief the children on the procedures of addressing all comments to the chair. You should choose to take a role yourself from which you can steer the debate from within. Allow them to enter the meeting room area gradually. Someone could be serving imaginary tea and coffee as they arrive, to add to the atmosphere. Such a debate could be a preliminary to listing the pros and cons of such developments, or writing letters of support or complaint.

Working from a script

Reading parts from scripts is one way of organising group reading. It can promote fluency and expression by justifying the re-reading process and giving a meaningful context to the reading. Where scripts have stage directions, this offers an additional opportunity to read for meaning, where the children are required to 'practise' the script and follow the stage directions as they do so.

Teacher in role

Several of the approaches which have been described so far have mentioned teacher in role. This can be a useful way to work because:

- it can help to direct the drama
- it can provide useful information for the children
- it enables you to model certain types of language
- it gives credibility to the power of pretence
- children usually enjoy having fun with their teacher!

Important guidance on how to maintain class control while in role is offered in Chapter 4, including clear boundaries between you and the role, use of props and positioning, directing from within, observing from within and so on.

 EXAMPLE

Writing to the sad toys

Time: 10 minutes role-play/20 minutes writing

Pretending that you are a postman/woman you explain that you are very concerned about the toys in the toy shop who have been upset because they never get any letters. In role you ask for volunteers to write to different toys (some of whom you might have brought along to introduce to the children).

 EXAMPLE

The Secret Garden

Time: 10 minutes video/20 minutes role-play

The children have been watching an excerpt from *The Secret Garden* (Warner Home Video UK Limited, 1994) and comparing it with a chapter in the book (Hodgson Burnett, first published in 1911, now available in Puffin, 1994). You explain that the author is going to travel in your class time machine to hear about their opinions of how the director has interpreted her book and made it into a film. Of course, she will be very shocked by the changes in the world since she died in 1924, especially the concept of film and sound.

Working with sound

Radio plays

The potential here is enormous – documentaries, plays, dramatised stories, interviews and so on. The planning should ideally follow on from improvisations. The beauty of sound only is that it can take place round a table in the classroom, and the eventual goal of taping then playing back the product is good for focusing children's minds! It is important to let children hear examples of the particular type of programme before expecting them to create something in the same genre. Creating sound effects and music is another enjoyable aspect of this approach.

 EXAMPLE

Making story tapes

Time: 10 minutes practice/5 minutes recording

Practising then recording individuals reading stories to be played back by other children in the listening-corner. Having an announcer adds a touch of fun and reality to this. Fluency and expression are important skills to practise, and recording adds motivation and a goal to the task.

 EXAMPLE

Jigsaw play

Time: 15 minutes whole class discussion/60 minutes planning and practice/ recording time

Different groups create radio plays, each group producing a different episode of the same which is agreed and established by the whole class first. This is great fun as each group has to recreate the same voices for characters. This can be a good platform for work on Standard English.

Detached voices

This approach is where one child speaks while another child presents physically. The voice might be behind a screen or shadowing the body. This can also be used to express the thoughts of a character.

 EXAMPLE

Puppet plays

Time: 10 minutes planning/5 minutes performance

Having chosen characters from a story and made lollipop stick puppets, the children take turns showing the story to the class, with some children operating puppets and others doing the voices. They can explore how many different versions of the story can be presented. The puppets need to follow the voices.

 EXAMPLE

Animal voices

Time: 10 minutes introduction/10 minutes planning/10 minutes sharing

Talk about animal characteristics. If they had voices what might they be like? What might they be like if one animal (e.g. a tiger) was interviewing another (e.g. a mouse) for a job? In fours, two animals and two voices plan a short scene of a job interview in which voices match actions.

Music as a stimulus

Inspiring music, rock, pop, electronic, classical, sad etc. can be a wonderful stimulus for discussion leading to tableaux and dance-drama.

Voices in tableaux

When using the tableau approach a complete change of dynamic can be introduced into the evaluations by inviting certain characters to give soundbites.

Stylised drama approaches

Mime

Situations are presented through actions and facial expression but without speech. This might be a single pupil presenting something for the rest of the class to guess, it might be a pair of pupils planning a sequence of events, or it could be a larger group showing a situation or story. In other words, it is an 'end product', just as a piece of writing or painting is the culmination of much useful preparatory planning, discussion, research and evaluation. These processes are the valuable part of the work. The mime itself can be the vehicle (i.e. the learning process) or the focus (i.e. the art form). Mime is also useful for encouraging children to pay attention to detail in communication.

 EXAMPLE
Favourite story characters

Time: 10 minutes

When recapping on the stories they have heard during the term, ask the children to think of their favourites. Ask individuals to mime their favourite characters for the others to guess, using either characteristic features of personality or specific actions relating to the story (or both).

 EXAMPLE
Scenes from Tudor life

Time: 15 minutes

As a consolidation process of work completed on this history theme, ask the children, in groups of five or six, to prepare a mime of a typical Tudor scene, including as much detail as possible. The rest of the class should describe what they think is happening, and the performing group should explain where they found their information.

Tableau

This is an immensely useful technique, because it makes very tightly structured demands of the children within a limited time frame, and yet it offers much scope for the development of their own ideas. A tableau is a still and silent scene or abstract representation of a theme created by a group of people. In a drama context, this group might be the whole class, where the children join the tableau one at a time as you build up an idea, event, or picture collaboratively. Alternatively, they might be working in groups of five or six to make a tableau, or sequence of tableaux. As this work takes place, they will be discussing ideas, possibly using books to discover information, planning, sequencing, evaluating, modifying and so on. The tableau approach can also be useful as a follow-on to guided imagery, where you have been asking the children to focus on a specific theme which they go on to discuss in groups, then present in this form. Much learning is taking place during the development process, and the finished product is the evidence of their work as an art form.

 EXAMPLE

Exploration of purposes for reading

Time: 5 minutes discussion/10 minutes tableaux examples

Discuss with the children how important reading is, and all the different reasons why children and adults read. In groups of three, ask them to make a tableau of a reading situation (e.g. library, newspaper on the bus, letter, teacher reading child's work etc.) for the rest of the class to guess. Give them just one minute to 'plan in secret' without the other groups hearing them. Remind them that because they won't be allowed to speak or move, they will need to give lots of clues with their positions and their faces!

 EXAMPLE

Greek mythology

Time: 30 minutes preparation/3 minutes per group showing time

Using their prior knowledge of Greek mythology, ask each group to select a particular story. They should read and research the story first, then plan three tableaux to present the key scenes or events. Each tableau could be linked by planned movement or music, if there was additional time for this.

Freeze-frame

When restructuring improvisations, the children could consider sometimes freezing the action for dramatic effect, perhaps accompanied by commentary or soundbites.

Dance-drama

Exploring and presenting themes or stories through movement can be an exciting and powerful way for children to work. Remember that they will need a lot of preparation work first.

 EXAMPLE

The exploding machine

Time: 15 minutes

Having built a machine of moving parts, where every child is a component and many components are connected in interesting ways, what happens to the machine if the speed is turned up too high and there is an explosion? Slow motion, use of levels, twisting, changing direction if they collide with another moving part etc.

KS2 EXAMPLE

The bully

Time: 10 minutes whole class discussion/20 minutes group work/15 minutes sharing

Read poem 'Duncan Gets Expelled' by Jackie Kay (1994). Discuss bullying and racism. Why? Who? Feelings? Solutions? In groups, the children create a movement piece to express mood and feeling. It can tell a story, but doesn't need to. Select good music for this.

Working towards performance

The notion of 'performance' takes us into a different emphasis for the drama. Rather than improvisational techniques which are not necessarily repeated, a performance is perhaps repeated several times, certainly in rehearsal. Although at one level it could be argued that a performance is for the benefit of the audience, in primary schools the processes involved in creating the performance are as important as the product itself. Initial exploratory drama techniques might be used in preparation for the performance, shaping ideas and storyline when there is no script as a starting point. Likewise, improvisations can assist the children in their understandings of characters with scripted drama. Such processes are important aspects of learning about communication in this art form.

Developing performance in schools is covered in more detail in Chapter 5 where theatre skills and practical knowledge are discussed. It is important to include performance as part of your planning for drama, included in either a discrete arts programme, as an extension of drama in English to develop communication skills, or simply to share the learning in other curricular areas. The performance element in itself exists along a continuum, from the simple showing of ideas, through repeated improvisation, structured improvisation, script production to fully rehearsed productions. Even the latter can be on a small or a grand scale. It will all depend on what is appropriate at the time. Puppets are a good example of this.

Puppet theatre

The making and using of puppets offers much to the primary curriculum. Benefits include:

- the exploration of language through play
- the shaping of story into performance
- the exploration and extension of known stories
- the creation of new stories
- associated technology activities (designing and making).

Puppets are particularly good for children who feel less confident about expressing themselves because the puppet is like a mask behind which they can hide. There is a distancing effect, which helps the work to feel safer, (which is why puppets are often used by psychologists with children who have been abused, to help them talk about difficult issues).

There are many ways of making puppets. For example:

- lollystick puppets – a card head with hair pasted to a flat lollipop stick
- paper bag puppets – draw a face on a white paper bag and use as a glove
- finger puppets – make a face or whole body in card and paste a card loop to the back so you can insert a finger. Several can be used by one person at the same time

- balloon heads – covering a balloon with papier mâché then fastening a stick below and covering with cloth
- plasticene modelling – design a head in plasticene, cover with papier mâché, attach cloth and use as a glove with fingers inside the head
- cloth puppets – attach cloth to a polystyrene ball
- shadow puppets – card silhouettes on thin sticks to play against a light, creating shadows on the wall
- commercial puppets – these are available everywhere from wildlife parks to toy shops, including string puppets, glove puppets, finger puppets etc
- reading scheme puppets – many publishers sell characters to accompany stories in their schemes.

Working towards a performance can be fun with puppets, but don't forget that they can also be used for language play and improvisation.

Summary

Many of the methods described in this chapter can be used either experientially, or as an expressive form, or both. The main difference between the two is that experiential work is usually not repeated, whereas performance is planned, shaped, rehearsed and presented. Sometimes it will be useful to the learning process to work towards performance and sometimes it will not. However, it is important not to forget that some opportunities for creative expression and performance of work must be built-in sometimes if children are to experience a truly balanced curriculum. If they do not have this opportunity, they are being deprived of the skills to express their ideas in extremely powerful and exciting ways.

New Wave Drama is about experience, reflecting on that experience, and sometimes performing in order to communicate the experience, which might be a story, an event, a collection of factual information, fantasy etc. Where appropriate contexts are used and the children are fully involved in the planning, design and delivery of a performance, there is much learning which can take place from working on a drama production.

Chapter 4

Management and Organisation

Few primary schools have, nor do they necessarily need, specialist facilities for the teaching of drama. Of the successful work seen, most took place in classrooms or halls.   (HMI 1990)

In this chapter you can read about:

- how the management of drama relates to different teaching styles
- the use of different group sizes
- the use of different spaces
- the importance of timing
- the teacher's role in drama
- some handy management techniques
- useful resources for drama.

The place of structure and organisation

The interactive and often open-ended nature of drama can understandably mislead sceptical observers into believing that such activities are disorganised. It is quite true that a drama activity which is not developed from sound planning and good management on the part of the teacher is in danger of leading to chaos, with very little real learning taking place, even if the children have a wonderful time! Just like other subjects taught in schools, drama has to be delivered with clear intentions about learning outcomes, and should operate within highly organised structures of management. These structures can range from tight teacher-led instructional approaches to child-led improvisations where the management is built into the preparation, the time allowed, the goals set and the reporting-back procedures.

Planning requires you to consider several different components. Firstly, the *content* which will be based upon curriculum requirements and your knowledge of the children's learning needs. Secondly, the *approach* (mode of drama) which will be based upon the content. Then, finally, you will need to think about the *organisation* of the session, which will require thinking about timing, groupings, space, resources and certain inbuilt teaching techniques which you can use to assist the management of the drama activity. It is this latter component, organisation, which we shall examine in this chapter.

Groupings for drama

It should be clear from reading Chapter 3 that the range of approaches to drama can require different types of groupings. The size and composition of a group influences the success of the work enormously, and careful thought needs to go into how these are created and why.

Group composition variables

Children can be grouped according to different criteria:

- ABILITY
  - *Same ability* e.g. to differentiate according to learning needs
  - *Mixed ability* e.g. to learn from others or learn from explaining to others

- AGE
  - *Similar age* e.g. to cater for age-related interest levels
  - *Different ages* e.g. to build in specific responsibilities

- GENDER
  - *Single gender* e.g. to cater for specific gender-related topics
  - *Mixed gender* e.g. more usual way of working

- SOCIAL SKILLS
  - *Confident/less confident* e.g. to enable less confident children to work without being dominated
  - *Mixed* e.g. to help focus on different roles within a (group leader, conciliator, critic etc.)

- FRIENDSHIP
  - *Children choosing* e.g. to develop an area of common interest
  - *Teacher Choosing* e.g. to 'break up' unproductive collaborations

- LANGUAGE
  - *Confident bilingual* e.g. where translations will broaden understanding and teach about language
  - *First Language* e.g. where children need to explore ideas in their first language before developing them in English

- SPECIALISMS
  - *Research* e.g. to work on an area of agreed common interest
  - *Expert* e.g. where certain 'specialisms' are needed within a group
  - *Generic* e.g. where several different specialisms are needed in each group (editor/illustrator/reporter etc.)

When applying such criteria to your decisions about groupings, you need to be sure that it will assist the learning process. You should also be careful not to reinforce implicit stereotypes into your groupings, particularly in single gender groups, (although *reversing* stereotypical roles can be a useful way to teach positively about issues of equal opportunities).

Group size

The size of a group makes a considerable impact upon the learning which takes place. In other areas of the curriculum, productivity is far higher where children are grouped at tables of four rather than six or eight. In drama, the interaction sometimes requires more than four. The group size also impacts upon the number of groups you will have to manage – it is far easier to work your way round four groups of eight than eleven groups of three – and this has major implications for your levels of input and feedback.

It is quite feasible for some drama activities to take place in smaller groups when the rest of the class are doing other things. (Art and drama go well together, and this has the added advantage of less clearing up if only half the class are using glue and paint!) In this case you need to relate your selection of group size to the level of teacher involvement required. For instance, two groups of six children developing a scripted improvisation from previous work carried out with you in the hall might only require occasional input and checking from you, working for the most part independently. On the other hand, exploratory work with the whole class, and you in role, clearly requires you to be there 100 per cent of the time!

The following guidance is intended to help you consider the advantages of different group sizes if you are new to teaching drama.

- *Pairs:* excellent for interviews, telephone conversations, question and answer sessions etc. Pair work is very suitable when working in a small area, or at tables in the classroom.

- *Trios:* adds the opportunity to have an observer to give feedback at the end, or a referee in a debate.
- *Fours:* useful when the children are working independently from you. Also good to bring two pairs into a group of four after working together on initial planning, or to swap partners for reporting back purposes.
- *Five/Six:* advisable to use these larger group sizes only when the children are able to work competently in drama, possibly reserving this approach until Key Stage 2. Larger groups like this are necessary where more characters are needed to create an improvisation or simulation.
- *Eight/Ten:* can work well with more structured activities (e.g. practising a scripted play). Advisable to have a designated leader for each group. High levels of teacher involvement are usually needed for larger groups.
- *Whole Class:* requires total teacher involvement, either through guided imagery (talking them through as individuals), or teacher-in-role during improvisation, simulation, etc.

Changing group size during the drama

It is sometimes appropriate and effective to reorganise the group sizes within the same drama activity so that the dynamics change to suit a particular stage of the process. Two examples of how this might happen are shown below.

EXAMPLE 1

Space voyage

(a) *Whole class/teacher's descriptive commentary:* individual mimes of putting on space equipment, walking in boots, testing controls etc., teacher operates this through a descriptive commentary
(b) *Pairs:* improvisations of checking equipment before take-off
(c) *Whole class/teacher-in-role:* exploring the planet where the craft has landed.

EXAMPLE 2

Introduction to topic about different foods

(a) *Whole class on carpet:* individually miming themselves eating a particular type of food for the teacher.
(b) *Pairs:* showing the mime to a partner and guessing.
(c) *Trios:* moving to tables, plan, then show a mime of preparing a particular food, (teamwork being essential!) giving lots of clues for others to guess.

Group splitting

Purposeful splitting of groups can be of great assistance to activities where you require children to report or explain. Here are some examples of this technique:

- *Partner swaps:* where the children work in pairs, then split up and find a new partner to report or ask questions.
- *Incremental Groups:* where smaller groups (e.g. pairs) are put together to form larger groups (e.g. into fours or sixes) in order to pool or compare ideas from their initial planning.
- *Rainbowing:* where the children work in one group, after which each child in the group is given a different colour. They then regroup into colour groups (with members of other groups), to report back, share, ask questions, seek information etc. This can be used as a device for moving

from expert groups to generic groups and vice versa.

- *Envoying:* where a member of each group moves to a central group to report or seek information (e.g. different groups representing members of a community each send a representative to a central committee to make a decision).

Using different spaces

In large schools, where hall use is limited to a twice-weekly slot, it is understandable that dance, PE and music take priority. However, this is no reason for not including drama in your weekly plans – hall space is not essential to drama. Of course, a large working space *is* sometimes needed, and this can be created elsewhere (even the playground can be appropriate sometimes). Here are some ideas about how you might use your own classroom for drama by rearranging the furniture:

- *Large space:* clear tables and chairs, either using a special team at playtime (before the lesson) and lunchtime (after the lesson), or 'training' the class in a drill-like manner, timing them each week to see if they can improve their record speed!
- *Carpet area:* if you have a carpeted reading corner in your classroom, this can be useful for introductory sessions, or showing work-in-progress/finished work. However, do bear in mind that when children have to sit in a cramped space for long periods they can become restless through no fault of their own – they are simply uncomfortable. If you know they will be sitting for longer than ten minutes, it is usually worth making a circle of chairs instead.
- *Role-play area:* as well as using this area for actual role-play, it can also be a handy space to use when children are preparing something in an independent group to show later to the rest of the class.
- *Tables and chairs:* the existing furniture in your classroom can be used to create all sorts of scenarios. Some examples are shown in Figure 4.1 overleaf. The moving of chairs and tables can help to solve the space problem, but also serves to create an illusion of a different place. This is usually very appealing to children and adds to the credibility of the drama.

The importance of timing

If you are planning a drama session which is likely to last for longer than half an hour, it is important to plan the how much you will allow for each of the different components (e.g. five minutes warm up, five minutes individual improvisation, ten minutes pair work, ten minutes reporting back). It is also essential that you always make time limits clear to the children. Prompts such as 'You have five minutes to create your tableaux.' and 'You have two minutes left.' all help to keep them on-task.

A certain amount of sensitive tuning is also vital. If children are left for too long on a particular activity they will usually become bored which inevitably leads to off-task behaviour. Don't be afraid to set additional challenges, go into role to change the way things are moving, or call the class back together for a reminder or review if you feel this is necessary. The unpredictability of some drama sessions requires that you may have to make changes to your original plans to enable the progress of the drama to lead to useful learning outcomes.

Another important point relating to time is that drama doesn't always need to take place as a long sustained session. Drama is a valuable tool to use throughout the week for all sorts of purposes, in addition to the specific 'drama lesson', and such inclusions can vary in the time taken from five to 35 minutes. A five minute mime can be a good introduction to a new science topic, researching from non-fiction books to create a tableau might be a ten minute task as part of a history activity and so on.

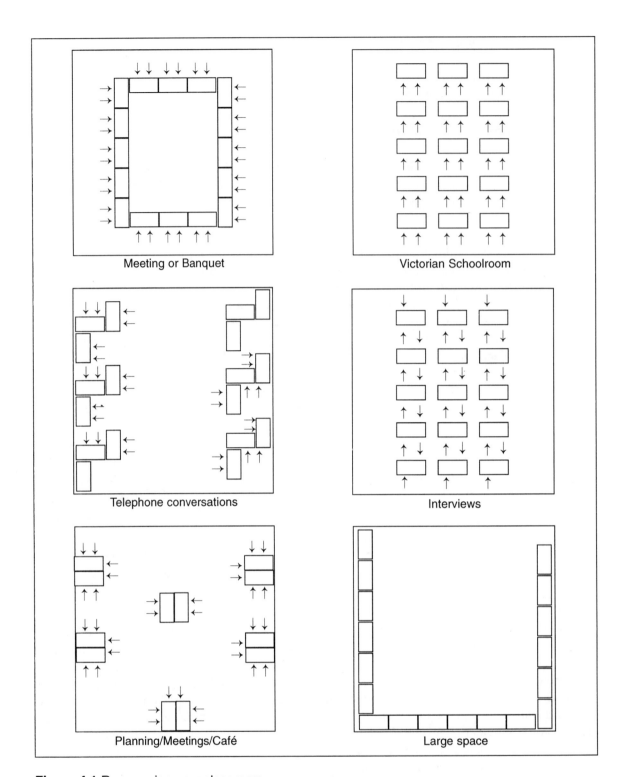

Figure 4.1 Rearranging your classroom

Meeting or Banquet

Victorian Schoolroom

Telephone conversations

Interviews

Planning/Meetings/Café

Large space

The role of the teacher

Even when you are not 'in role' you have many roles to play! Perhaps these might be better described as responsibilities. They include:

- providing the necessary information, examples and resources to help the children's understanding
- showing them that you are prepared to take part in the make-believe
- explaining in ways which can be understood by all
- making clear your expectations and setting challenging but achievable targets
- giving feedback throughout
- listening to the children's ideas and points of view
- ensuring that everyone has equal opportunities
- allowing time for children to reflect and evaluate.

When you take on a role as part of the actual drama, your relationship with the children changes. It is therefore important to use management techniques which help you to maintain control despite the altered dynamic. It is helpful to remember the following rules of thumb:

1. *Make firm divisions between you as teacher and you as the character.*
   Agree a clear signal to indicate when you are in role and when you are not (e.g. 'When I am sitting on that chair, I am the angry police inspector, but when I am on this chair I am back to being me.').
2. *Enter into the spirit of the pretend according to your ability.*
   Try to use voice and posture to create your role, but don't worry if you feel you can't act. The children will absolutely love the fact that you are joining in the pretend, and will not be making judgements about your performance.
3 *Use what you can to help you.*
   Additional props or pieces of costume such as a hat or a shawl can help to create the illusion, and will also give you more confidence if you do feel a bit nervous. These can become part of the de-roling signal if you wish, (i.e. 'When I take the hat off I am back to being me!').
4 *Remember that you can control from within the role.*
   A character can change the direction of the drama, so if the 'crowd' are wandering around aimlessly, you as 'irate townswoman' can leap onto your soap box and say, 'I am absolutely fed up of all this filth and disease. What we need round here are some decisions. Who is going to see the mayor about these rats?'.

Working in role can operate at different levels. For instance, you might be in a controlling role (e.g. the Pied Piper) steering the drama from within, or you might be an observer (e.g. one of the following children). The level of input will vary according to the type of activity, the experience of the children and the nature of the content. It is certainly helpful to clarify the function of your input in your own mind when planning the session, but also remember that you might need to change or add to this during the drama if the need arises. Figure 4.2 shows examples of the main functions of teacher-in-role.

Teacher techniques

With years of experience, good teachers develop a repertoire of techniques which they know are effective when managing a class. New teachers can be helped by learning such techniques from sound advice, rather than expecting them to evolve through trial and error! However, the techniques outlined here are not intended as a definitive magical list, but rather as a useful starting point. Hopefully, this will give you the confidence to develop your own preferred adaptations of these approaches, by trying other ideas of your own.

FUNCTION OF THE ROLE	EXAMPLES OF TEACHER'S ROLE
To set a problem or challenge...	In role as a toy shop owner who keeps finding the toys in all the wrong places each morning.
To provide information...	In role as an escapee from a volcanic eruption where there are still people to be rescued.
To act as a go-between...	In role as a teddy bear who can talk to the organisers of a picnic on behalf of the other bears.
To lead...	In role as the lead investigator of a robbery.
To intervene...	In role as a 'boss' when the arguments between factory workers become too circuitous.
To rescue...	In role as a new character bringing additional information when the drama becomes 'stuck'.
To model...	in role as a politician in the House of Commons.
To bring things to an end...	In role as a caretaker, saying it is time for the meeting to finish, and asking them to decide if and when they need to meet again.

Figure 4.2 Functions of teacher in role

Developing working rules

Establishing clear working rules helps the drama to succeed because the children are clear about what is expected of them. It is better to have just a small number of rules which can be remembered and wherever possible these should be developed with the children themselves. In this way they will have ownership of the rules and will also be more likely to remember them. Questions such as: 'When you are working in groups how will you let the others know you want to say something?', 'If you disagree with someone's idea, how is the best way to tell them?', actually encourage children to consider the reasons for the rules as well as the actual rules themselves.

Stopping and starting the action

When 35 children are all enthusiastically discussing and planning, there is usually noise. Shouting over such noise can often result in raising the noise level rather than reducing it. There are certain techniques which you can build in to your way of working which will help you to maintain good control. Here are some suggestions:

- *Magic cushion/control chair*
  Select a special chair or cushion and place it in a prominent spot in the room. Explain to the children that when you sit on the chair it is your signal to them that it is time for a discussion, and they should gather round quickly and quietly, sitting on the floor around you ready to listen. Praise them for arriving quickly, and sitting quietly.

- *Group gathering*
  If the class are all working simultaneously in groups, it is sometimes better to gather each group separately rather than calling the whole class at once. This can be done by visiting the groups first which seem to be near completion. Ask them about their work then instruct them to join you by the control chair. As these groups gradually move to the space and sit down, the others will become aware that work has stopped and so will join the rest.

- *Sound signals*

  A chime, shake of the tambourine, beat of the drum, chord on the piano etc. can be a signal to stop working and listen without moving away from their work space. An agreed sound like this is far better than shouting over the tops of busy talking voices. Older children should be able to respond to different signals, for example, a chime meaning stand still/stop talking, a tambourine meaning sit on the floor/stop talking, three drum beats meaning freeze, a chord on the piano meaning gather round on the carpet etc.

- *Countdown*

  Counting down from five or ten can be a good way to focus children's attention. The countdown might be a signal to a point at which they freeze ('…three, two, one, freeze!'), or it can also be a signal for action to begin ('…three, two, one, ACTION!'). Changing the volume of your voice so it becomes louder as a build-up to action, or quieter as it focuses down to stillness adds further control.

Movement and stillness

Stillness can be as effective as movement. It is also a part of 'controlling' the drama. The following key techniques can be useful to use within different drama methods, and children should be taught to respond to these in the very early stages.

- *Freeze*

  To freeze is to become still instantly and hold the position like a statue. It is important to teach children how to freeze properly by explaining that *everything* is still, including eyes and lips. It is also advisable to teach them not to focus their gaze on another person, as this can distract them and disturb the stillness.

- *Slow motion*

  Moving in slow motion (like action replays on televised football) can bring dramatic focus to a performance, and can also be an exciting way to control the action. Modelling this for the children can help them to understand that even blinking and turning the head have to be at a reduced speed. Slow motion can be a good way of linking sections of a drama (e.g. a journey back through time), and can also be useful for moving in and out of role (e.g. from a freeze position at the end of a piece to sitting on the carpet ready for discussion).

- *Choreographed movement*

  When children need to link pieces together, e.g. a set of three tableaux, they should have the opportunity to plan their movements carefully. One framework for this is to ask them to plan the changeover in four separate movements, providing four drum beats to assist the process. Encourage them to work as a team, making links between their movements so that they create interesting shapes and directions.

Making time for all

If all children are to feel that their work is valued and are to have the opportunity to perform and receive feedback it is important that no-one is omitted. However, often time can run out and you are left with the problem of how to give the activity a satisfactory conclusion. There are certain management techniques which can be used to help solve this problem.

One to one

When 35 children sitting on the carpet all eagerly want to show their mime or share an idea, it can sometimes help to let them show a partner (simultaneously) so they at least have the opportunity to express themselves and receive some feedback.

Group to group

If you have six groups, divide them into three lots of two and let them perform simultaneously to their partner group. You should circulate round all three and ensure that you can say something about each at the end.

Rotating the days

When children are working in smaller groups towards a performance of their work, it can be appropriate to allow them to do this on different days. This helps solve the problem of space and also means that the presentation of their work can be spaced out during the course of the week.

Teacher envoys

Select an individual child to watch each group as if they are the teacher, making it clear to everyone that at the end these envoys will each take a turn to report back to the whole class on what they have seen.

Calming down time

Children might need to calm down at the beginning of a session, for example if they have just come in from playtime, and they will always need to calm down and de-role at the end of the session. Not only is it disturbing for other classes to be interrupted by 36 Viking warriors rampaging back to their classroom, it is also going to affect the next learning activity if children's minds and bodies are still full of the drama. In some cases, such as one in which you have been dealing with more disturbing issues, it is also vital that the children have the opportunity to 'let go' of that and feel safe in the knowledge that they are now back in the normal school situation.

There are several techniques which you can use as calming and de-roling exercises. If there is enough space, let the children lie down and close their eyes. If not, let them sit comfortably with their eyes closed, out of reach of any other person. These are all tried and tested methods, used with all ages from four to sixty four! They do work!

- *Breathing and relaxation:* Ask them to focus their minds on the in-breath and the out-breath, counting silently to four on each out-breath, then starting again. If any thoughts distract them, ask them to let go of each thought as if it is a balloon floating away and start the counting again from one.

- *Body relaxation:* Ask them to focus their thoughts on their feet. Make their feet feel heavy, relaxed, sinking into the floor. Next the ankles, and so on, right through the body until the whole body is relaxed.

- *Guided meditation:* Once the children are comfortable and quiet, talk them through an imagined scene, e.g. 'Try to picture a beautiful beach. You are lying on the beach. You can hear the waves gently lapping on the shore…' etc. Take them through a calming journey which eventually leads them back to the classroom.

- *De-roling:* While the children sit with their eyes closed, summarise where they have just finished, then talk them back into the school situation. Then, explain what they are going to do next, e.g. 'When you get back to the classroom I would like you to get out your pencil and your maths book and finish the work on money which we started this morning.'. Ask them to open their eyes, and in a very quiet voice, ask them how they should return to the classroom, and what they will do when they get there. Tell them that you are going to watch them closely to see how well they can get on with your request.

Useful resources for drama

It is a good idea to build up a collection of props in your classroom in addition to the resources you might include in a role play area. Older children also love to have the added dimension of a prop or costume, so a special box of props should be considered for all classrooms, not just Key Stage 1. The purpose of these is not for large-scale productions but rather to assist and support children in their improvisations and role-play, or for you to use sometimes when you are taking on a role. The smallest item can help a child's imagination and confidence enormously. Here is a list of suggestions to get you started:

- dressing-up clothes
- hats
- telephones
- handbags
- newspapers and magazines
- pots and pans
- plants, ornaments, clock etc.
- supermarket basket
- empty cereal packets, tins, sauce bottles etc.
- tablecloth
- crockery and cutlery
- walking stick
- briefcase
- suitcase
- masks
- puppets.

It is also useful to have the following readily available:

- sound effect tapes
- tape recorder
- musical instruments
- storage boxes
- hanging rail
- rostra of various shapes and sizes.

N.B. Car boot sales are an excellent place to find many of these items, especially telephones!

Chapter 5

Theatre Arts and English

A drama education which begins with play may eventually include all the elements of theatre. Like all the arts, drama helps us to make sense of the world.   (Arts Council, 1992)

This chapter includes:

- a consideration of the place of theatre arts in the primary curriculum
- a suggested relationship between theatre arts and the rest of the curriculum
- introductory guidelines on theatre skills and crafts
- suggested ways of working with theatre professionals
- an outline of desired critical responses
- a glossary of theatre terms for children to use.

A new wave of theatre arts

Chapter 1 describes how New Wave Drama embraces theatre arts in ways which have rarely been seen before in primary education, combining with the more traditional experiential drama approaches to provide a balanced and integrated approach to drama. This chapter aims to offer you support with more specialist knowledge that has not always been addressed in the past by some educational drama books, which have tended to focus just on the 'processes' of learning through drama.

The statutory requirement for theatre arts

Chapter 2 outlines the ways in which drama is a component of the core requirements of the National Curriculum. Drama as a whole is required to be taught by law, as outlined in the statutory Order for English (1995). In addition to the implicit usefulness of drama as a process by which children can learn and practise interactive language skills, there is an explicit requirement within the Order to include elements of theatre arts in the primary curriculum (see Figure 2.1, p6 and Figure 2.2, p7).

At Key Stage 1: 'Pupils should be encouraged to participate in drama activities, improvisation and performances of varying kinds, using language appropriate to a role or situation. They should be given opportunities to respond to drama they have watched, as well as that in which they have participated.' (Para. 1d, p. 3.)

At Key Stage 2: 'Pupils should be given opportunities to participate in a wide range of drama activities, including improvisation, role play, and the writing and performing of scripted drama. In responding to drama, they should be encouraged to evaluate their own and others' contributions.' (Para. 1d, p. 9.)

In these extracts, the use of the terms 'performance' and 'scripted drama' suggest activities which are more closely aligned to theatrical objectives than the process learning associated with unrepeated improvisational-type drama. In other words, it is requiring activities where the aim is to work with ideas and texts to present to an audience. This is a most welcome inclusion in the National Curriculum as it gives teachers a clear mandate to provide appropriate theatre-based activities within a wider Expressive Arts curriculum.

Expressive Arts in the primary school

Drama, Music, Art and Dance are sometimes referred to as the Performing Arts. However, in primary education it is more appropriate to use the term Expressive Arts, which encompasses a more integrated arts approach and also includes writing. Performance' skills, although they have some part to play in young children's education, are quite subject-specific and specialist, whereas 'expressive' skills are more transferable and can be used for the exploration, development and communication of thoughts and ideas.

The 1988 Education Act states that all children have an entitlement to a 'broad and balanced curriculum'. The arts are part of life, and if the primary curriculum is to reflect truly a broad and balanced approach to life then it must, by default, include a comprehensive arts programme. The arts, on one level, are a source of enjoyment, challenge and recreation – a part of life which is separate from work, (apart from for those who work in the arts industry). On another level, they are engines of cultural transmission – the transmission of stories, emotions, philosophies, ideas, belief systems and change which are part of the fabric of society itself. If children are denied access to all this, they are missing not only the chance to express themselves through such channels but also the means to enjoy and appreciate the work of others, now and in the future.

All children need to be given the opportunity to develop an awareness of the very existence of the arts, an understanding of the ways in which they communicate their stories and messages, and an enjoyment of the sheer pleasures they have to offer. This in turn can provide them with the skills to express their own ideas through these media, and to recognise their entitlement to continue to understand and enjoy arts activities and events beyond school and into adulthood.

Theatre and the Expressive Arts

Theatre has always had a central social role to play in the lives of human beings, evidence of which goes right back to the Ancient Greeks. Apart from the period from 1642 to 1660 when the Puritans succeeded in closing down English theatres, there has been a strong tradition of theatre in Britain, always reflecting the moods and ideas of the times. Medieval Mystery Plays, Elizabethan travelling players performing Shakespeare, Restoration comedy, Victorian melodrama and later Victorian political drama all paved the way to the tapestry of theatrical genres available today – musical, farce, comedy, kitchen-sink drama, pyscho-drama, political and social drama and so on. Likewise, in other parts of the world there is a rich variety of theatre, from the tragi-comedy of Chekhov in Russia to Aboriginal representations of the Dreamtime.

Of all the arts subjects, theatre arts lend themselves to the integration of arts subjects most naturally. In the primary school, the preparations and performance can include music, dance and art, craft and design as a holistic part of the drama. This does not necessarily mean that the other arts subjects should always be 'driven' by the drama, never standing alone in their own right. Far from it. But it does mean that planning for theatre arts in the primary school can provide golden opportunities for making meaningful contexts for the other arts subjects. Indeed, it can also provide a fruitful vehicle for the exploration and delivery of other curriculum areas.

Theatre arts and the whole curriculum

Other subjects in the curriculum, including arts subjects, can be used in conjunction with theatre arts in two ways – as curriculum content or curriculum application.

Curriculum content

This approach is where the content matter of a curriculum area is used as all or part of the subject matter for the drama. Examples of this might include:

English: KS1 – dramatisation of story into puppet theatre
              KS2 – working with extracts from Shakespeare

Science: KS1 – dance-drama of the life cycle of plants
              KS2 – the environmental impact of disturbing the food chain

History: KS1 – the life story of a famous character
              KS2 – myths and legends of ancient Greece

Geography: KS1 – a visit to a farm or a city
              KS2 – a town divided by opinion about a new motorway

Curriculum application

This approach is where the skills from a curriculum area are applied generically to the overall planning, preparation and performance of the drama. Examples of this might include:

Maths: KS1 – numbering, sorting or counting of tickets
              KS2 – calculating income from ticket sales/translating scales of designs

Design and   KS1 – designing, making and evaluating props
Technology: KS2 – designing, making and evaluating models for sets and scenery

ICT: KS1 – word processing script soundbites
              KS2 – designing tickets

Art: KS1 – graphic design of posters, after looking at the work of professionals
              KS2 – creating scenery from models, after looking at the work of professionals

Music: KS1 – singing songs from memory, developing control of breathing, dynamics, rhythm and pitch
              KS2 – rehearsing and presenting pupil compositions

Dance: KS1 – exploring moods and feelings, using rhythmic responses and contrasts of speed, shape, direction and level
              KS2 – creating simple characters and narratives

All these examples relate directly to the stated requirements in the National Curriculum Orders for each subject. Not only do they illustrate the scope for using performance as a context for applying a range of skills, they also show how the National Curriculum can be planned creatively in ways which will motivate children by providing a purposeful context, and in doing so, help them learn more effectively.

Theatre skills and crafts

Never underestimate the ability of children to learn new skills, especially when they are connected with drama, film and television! You will usually find that the children are extremely motivated to learn and try new techniques because they are such fun and also because the application of skills and knowledge to the creation of performance makes such a noticeable impact upon all those involved. Acknowledging and developing theatre skills and crafts in your work with children, where appropriate, is giving full respect to drama as an expressive art, and providing useful techniques which enhance learning. However, it is important to achieve a balance. Over-emphasis on skills can become tedious and inappropriate. Lack of emphasis on skills can mean that children do not have the tools to create powerful drama for communication – this can lead to frustration and boredom.

Acting

Improvisation undoubtedly helps children to develop understanding of characters, and this can be a good way to prepare children for a part. Indeed, many professional directors put their actors through the paces of improvising different perspectives on a scene before moving into the scripted version. In school you might be using the improvisation as material for a script anyway.

Here are some simple key starting points to guide you through the sorts of things you might 'teach' about acting. Of course they can all be taught in varying degrees, according to the age of the children, so your interpretation of the first bullet point could range between, 'If you are skipping on to the stage, the audience will see that you are happy. Skip on and try to show me how happy you are.', to, 'How can we show the audience by the way you move that you are sad as you walk across the stage?'. The aim of acting is to create believability for the audience, and that is the main emphasis which you should always place on skills development with children, that they are taking part in building an artistic 'illusion', rather than training to become star turns!

- Movement affects the audience's perception of the character by creating visual images.
- Stillness can also be used for dramatic effect.
- The voice can be used in many different ways, and the expression tells part of the story.
- The voice needs to project so the audience can hear.
- Speaking too quickly will distort the sound. (Children tend to rush to get their bit over with! They will need practice in slowing down. Over-emphasising this can sometimes help.)
- Pauses are as important as speaking sometimes.
- Physical gesture (e.g. folding arms if on the defensive, scratching nose if nervous etc.) can add to the drama.
- Props can also be used to provide physical gestures (e.g. fiddling with an ornament at an awkward point).
- The relationships between the characters can be shown in speech and actions.
- Lines spoken are driven by a thought in the character's head (motivation).
- Encourage children not to look at the audience. It destroys the 'pretence', and also puts them off if they see someone they know!

Directing

The way in which you direct children, if you are working towards a class performance for assembly or for a production will totally affect the development of their confidence. If you shout at them and criticise them for making mistakes they will very likely become increasingly nervous about the whole thing. Make it enjoyable, don't be afraid to repeat things, giving lots of encouragement each time, plus an additional focus for next time. Here are some simple guidelines.

- Be careful not to typecast children into roles which may reinforce features which are sensitive.
- If you have to audition, treat this with sensitivity, ensuring that every child gets a part and is told about the positive things which they have to offer to this part.
- Show that you value everyone, especially the small players. 'Guards, you stood really still during that scene, and you looked very stern. Well done. It's not easy to stand still for so long!'
- Make sure there are no stars or prima donnas!
- Explain and use technical language appropriate to the age (see the glossary at the end of this chapter). Children will soon acquire this new vocabulary, especially if they hear you repeating it often.
- Rehearse in small chunks first. These can be repeated in fun ways to help teach and consolidate, rather than doing too much which the children then forget.
- Only start to piece together the larger total towards the end when they are feeling confident.
- Improvise small sections to help the children understand situations and characters.
- Give clear instructions about where to move and when.
- Weave in as many of the children's own ideas as you can. Help them to feel that it is their work. Always be open to suggestions.
- Don't be afraid to demonstrate!
- Make notes during rehearsals to feed back to individuals.
- Teach the children not to turn their back on the audience unless it is for dramatic effect.
- Stand at the back of the hall so they have to project their voices. If you sit at the front they will talk to the front.
- Tell them how their work makes you feel.

Rehearsals

Rehearsals should be well planned to avoid children getting bored and the whole process becoming a chore. Several practical suggestions might help you here.

- If it is an extra-curricular production, provide a clear rehearsal timetable for every child. Different scenes on different days, with a list of who is required, and when. Also include the technical rehearsal and the dress rehearsal.
- If it is part of your class work, it can still be good to pin up a schedule. This also enables you to model writing for this purpose, encourages the children to read for information and helps you to plan the time needed.
- Only rehearse for short periods, especially with infants. Better to repeat a little several times and enable them to enjoy the praise of success than to practice a long stretch which they will not retain.
- Sub-contract sections to be rehearsed without you (e.g. small group of infants with another adult, older children with a group director in the reading corner).
- Never ridicule their mistakes.

Designing

Designing a set for a play provides opportunities for the development of art and technology skills. The stages of design can include:

- preliminary sketches
- floor plans
- models
- final construction.

The children can be involved at different levels, but it is clear that there is much scope for cross-curricular work here. Designing and interpreting floor plans for instance is a wonderfully practical and purposeful way of teaching mapping skills for geography.

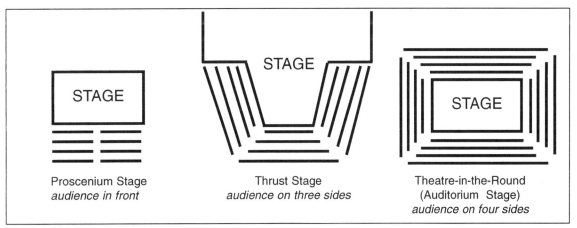

Figure 5.1 Placing the audience

Sets can be divided into two types. **Symbolic sets** are simple sets where things are just represented symbolically. **Realistic sets** are where you aim to create the illusion of reality, such as a room. Sets might be interior or exterior and you need to consider how scene changes will happen if appropriate. Clearly, scene design can only be discussed briefly here, but the following suggestions offfer some practical advice:

- Different levels can create visual interest.
- Rostra do not always need to be parallel or at right angles to the audience.
- The audience can be placed in various positions.
- Walls and climbing bars can be disguised with fabric.
- Camouflage nets create wonderful effects, especially for forests.
- Try to use real furniture rather than dressing up school chairs and tables.
- Shops will usually help to lend furniture and props, providing you acknowledge them in the programme.
- Parents will also be a willing source, for artefacts and practical help.
- Screens can be useful to hide characters.
- Check to see if any scenery is casting shadows.
- Block off any view of backstage activities. The sight of children jumping up and down while waiting to go on is very distracting for the audience!

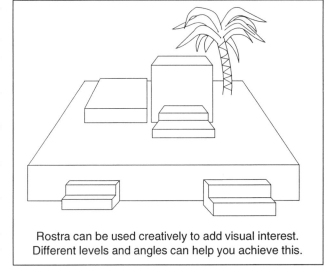

Rostra can be used creatively to add visual interest. Different levels and angles can help you achieve this.

Figure 5.2 Using levels and angles

Sound

Additional sound can be used for a variety of reasons as part of a performance, and there are different ways of achieving effects for different purposes. Sound production can be divided broadly into three categories:

1. *Atmospheric sound* – to help create a mood, for example points of tension or humour, e.g. pathos music as Cinderella is left alone to scrub the floor.

2. *Functional sound* – which is almost like a prop to help the drama and create the illusion of reality, e.g. a telephone ringing.
3. *Sound markers* – to act as boundaries or signals, e.g. music at the end of the first half to signal the interval.

In school performances it is quite appropriate to use commercially produced sound, music and effects, with permission from the copyright holder (the BBC produces excellent tapes of sound effects from creaking doors to seaside beaches). However, it is also good to involve the children in sound making as well, either live during the performance or recorded on tape. Clearly, there is an enormous amount of scope for composition and performance as outlined in the National Curriculum Order for music. Wherever possible, the children should be involved in the decision-making, development and production of the sound. Older children could even take on the role of conductor during the performance. Other useful things to remember are:

- for live sound or the use of recordings, the children should follow a cue sheet which tells them when to come in
- use good quality speakers and place them where they won't dominate the actors' voices
- use a tape recorder which has a counter to help identify cues
- always make a backup tape
- always have a technical rehearsal as well as a dress rehearsal
- always keep a spare tape recorder in reserve
- always check the tape before a performance
- play appropriate music before the performance to set the mood – also during any interval and afterwards.

Lighting

Controlling the lighting in a production can make an enormous difference to the moods and atmospheres. Some schools are equipped with spotlights in the hall, but others have to hire lighting. If neither of these options is possible in your school, or if your performance is only a small-scale production (e.g. class assembly or a showing to another class) it is quite possible to change the lighting in ways which will convince the children that they are doing something special and also create enhancing effects for the audience.

Professional light hire

There are companies which hire out lighting equipment. Indeed, many theatres hire rather than buy their own lights, or hire additional specialised resources for specific productions. It is beyond the scope of this book to even outline all you need to know about this very skilled job. It is advisable to involve someone who knows something about lighting and electrics if you are new to stage lighting, or certainly read more specialised information. However, there are one or two basic principles which can be outlined here. For instance, every light casts a shadow. You therefore need to balance the lighting from all sides to eliminate unwanted shadows. Lights from above cast different shadows on the actors' faces than lights shining upwards from the floor and so on.

Stage lights are usually high voltage and get very hot indeed, so safety is a big issue. Suspended lights should always have a safety chain, and freestanding lights should always be weighted down and have a prohibited area all around them. Children should *never* be allowed close to freestanding spotlights. Connecting leads should always be taped to the floor.

One of the most useful pieces of equipment is a dimmer board. This has sliding switches which will dim one light or a group of lights, depending on what you connect to it. The more modern computerised dimmer boards can enable you to plan lighting changes digitally, so at the press of a switch, one group of lights might go down while a different set come up. If you are not hiring lights, you may still find it useful to visit a theatrical light hire company to buy gels. These are coloured celluloid sheets which can be cut to fit over lights to create a special effect. There are over 80 different colours available and they can be used singly or in combination to mix colours. Most useful are:

No. 3	Straw	warm, sunny
No. 6	Primary Red	sunsets, fire
No. 20	Deep Blue	cold, water
No. 39	Primary Green	forest
No. 37	Pale Lavender	natural light
No. 53	Pale Salmon	fairyland, rosy glow
No. 63	Sky Blue	sky

If you are not using professional lighting, these gels can be used with more everyday resources as suggested below.

Home-made lighting effects
There is much you can create from resources you already have. Here are some useful examples:

- use coloured gels over the auditorium lights
- turn off the hall lights over the audience but not over the acting area
- overhead projectors can be used (with or without gel) to create a local pool of light
- desk lamps can be directed towards spots and moved around
- torches can be shone from the wings or by the actors themselves
- coloured light bulbs can be bought from most hardware shops
- table lamps strategically placed can create a different effect
- household dimmer switches can be wired into a connector board to plug in your lamps.

Vary the lighting to mark a change of scene or mood (e.g. hall lights off/torches on). Sudden change can have an impact on the audience. Also, be sure to give status to the lighting technicians and provide them with clipboards and cue sheets. They should also be responsible for running checks before the performance.

Make-up

There are really only two main reasons for using stage make-up. Firstly, to change the appearance of the actor (e.g. to make them look older), and secondly to counteract the draining effects of bright stage lights. If you are not using stage lighting, you should not need to use make-up unless it is to create characters. Masks are also a useful way of achieving this effect.

The use of make-up needs design and application knowledge. There are also important hygiene factors to be considered. Here are some useful pointers:

- Check children for allergic reactions.
- Clean sticks before using them on a new person (and check for infectious skin conditions).
- A towel around the neck and shoulders, and headband to hold back hair, are essential.
- A base of moisturiser or cold cream should always be applied before using stage make-up.
- Use the child's natural lines (e.g. for grumpy character, ask child to frown and follow their natural frown lines to apply the wrinkles).
- Dark shades create hollows and depth, light shades bring the face outwards, so to make a nose appear thinner, apply shadows down each side and light make-up down the ridge.
- Eyebrows often need accentuating.
- Apply fixing-powder with cotton wool to prevent the stage paint from melting.
- Remove make-up with cold cream before trying to wash.
- Wigs make a dramatic difference to appearance, even those which are home-made from wool or curled paper.

Box office

The making and selling of tickets for a performance offers golden opportunities for involving the children in useful learning tasks. The three advantages to this are:

1. It gives them a sense of ownership and responsibility
2. It offers maths opportunities with a real-life context
3. It saves you having to do it!

Box office activities might include planning the size and design of the tickets (how many to a sheet of A4), planning the auditorium layout (how many chairs to a row/how many rows), numbering rows and tickets, calculating prices and selling tickets, giving change etc. Two box office managers could be selected each day, ten minutes before the start of school, to sell tickets to parents, keep a tally and total up the money. This could be simplified for infants by getting them to keep a tally sheet, and ensuring that the ticket prices are simple, easy figures.

Publicity

Likewise, the design of posters, photographic displays for the 'foyer' and programmes can provide excellent learning activities. The programme in particular offers scope for different styles of writing (advertisements, actor profiles, synopsis, scene list etc.). As with all writing and art activities, it is important to show the children examples of professional posters and programmes before expecting them to embark upon their own ideas. Reproducing a programme which includes a piece of work from every child is a tremendous endorsement of purpose, and there is no doubt that the children will be thrilled to see the mass production and sale of their efforts!

Working with professionals

As with most areas of work in the primary school, it is an extremely valuable part of their learning for the children to meet and work with professional adults in the field. Most theatres have an Education Officer whose job it is to help you enable this to happen with maximum impact. Visits to see performances are the obvious starting point, and indeed it is stated clearly in the Order for English that this should happen. It is not unreasonable to apply a school policy of one theatre trip per term for all classes. This enables you to plan for a wide range of performances, for example pantomime, dramatisation of children's literature, appropriate topical drama, puppet shows, mime, ballet, contemporary dance and so on. If children are only ever taken to pantomimes they are likely to develop a very limited perception of theatre, so it is vital that they are exposed to a *range* if they are to develop truly discerning skills of critical response.

Theatre companies come in all shapes and sizes – national, local, touring and theatre in education (TIE). It is also worth remembering that many other organisations also offer theatrical experiences, for example the National Trust, stately homes such as Warwick Castle, and some museums. When taking children to a theatre, it is often possible to arrange backstage tours, either in addition to seeing the performance or as a separate visit. This enables them to talk to a whole range of people working in the theatre – wardrobe manager, stage technician, make-up artists, director, theatre manager, box office manager and so on, in addition to the actors. Both a performance and a tour require a certain level of preparation beforehand. The more the children know before the visit, the more they will be able to ask appropriate questions in order to extend their learning.

It is also possible to work with professionals in schools. Many TIE companies work 'on the road', performing and working with children in workshops. These workshops can be with small groups, whole classes, or even the whole school, and might involve exploring themes, explaining their work or developing new drama with the children. The Learning Through Action Trust is a splendid organisation which works with children (and runs courses for teachers) both in schools and back at their base in Reading. They provide experiential workshops on historical topics, and also specialise in working with children who have behavioural difficulties (see Appendix 2 for details).

Visiting experts

Likewise it is possible to invite individual adults into school to talk about their work, or to run workshops. Some puppeteers, for instance, will put on a performance, then run a workshop on making puppets. Mime artists also sometimes offer this option. Alternatively, you may wish to invite in an actor or designer to talk about his or her work and answer the children's questions.

Professional resources

Other useful support for drama can be found in resource packs. Film Education will send you superb activities for children linked to films – and they are free! The RSC Education Department produces good information packs at secondary level, but not much at primary level at the moment. However, this information can be an excellent resource for developing your own knowledge of approaches to productions of Shakespeare, which you in turn can adapt for your own age group.

There are many other types of resources available to teachers from theatres, which can also be used in the classroom. Used tickets, programmes, posters, set design plans, costume drawings and photographs can usually be obtained if you build up a good contact with your nearest theatre. These are enormously useful for children to look at and discuss when they are working on their own designs. Information and resource packs are also available from many theatres, particularly larger theatres which have Arts Council funding for that purpose. (Funding can also be used to sponsor special projects in schools such as Theatre in Residence.) It is surprising how much free information and resource material is available if you only know where to look! The list of useful addresses and telephone numbers given in Appendix 2 has been provided to help you.

Developing critical responses

The Programmes of Study for Drama, published by the Arts Council in 1992 in a booklet called *Drama in Schools*, outline three areas of assessment in the End of Key Stage Statements – Making, Performing and Responding. (The full Programmes of Study for Key Stages 1 and 2 can be found in Appendix 3 of this book, and are discussed in more detail in Chapter 10.) Responding to drama, both that of others and also their own, is an important part of children's learning and development. The requirement to respond focuses their observations, and the requirement to communicate those responses involves the organisation and externalisation of thoughts and ideas. Watching a play may be an enjoyable experience, but going on to reflect upon and discuss that experience is helping to develop skills of oracy and literary analysis, both important parts of the English curriculum.

Evaluating and reflecting upon their own performances in schools is a vital part of ongoing development and progression. Evaluating and reflecting upon professional performances is also valuable because it provides a tremendous variety of experiences to which children (and adults) can respond – different actors, characters, costumes, set design, scenery changes, music, lighting, sound effects, audience reaction and so on. The provision of all this material at a professional level will extend children's expectations of what is possible and help them to develop a language of response which they can also use when talking about their own work.

There are five types of response which can encompass a wide range of subjects. Examples are given at each key stage, but you should recognise that the range within each type of response is enormous. 'Giving an Opinion', for instance, could be about the way the play ends, a particular actor's performance, the choice of music and so on. The categorisation of these response types is intended to help your awareness of the possibilities.

Giving an opinion	KS1 – describing a part which they did or did not enjoy
	KS2 – agreeing/disagreeing with a character portrayal
Justifying opinion	KS1 – saying why they did not like a certain character
	KS2 – giving examples of contradictory character behaviour
Drawing comparisons	KS1 – comparing a character's behaviour with a real life example
	KS2 – comparing a production with a TV version of the same
Offering Alternatives	KS1 – suggesting different ideas for costume designs
	KS2 – suggesting alternative interpretations of text
Empathising	KS1 – describing how a character felt at a certain point
	KS2 – describing character motivation for certain action

To elicit such responses and nurture an ethos in which children feel empowered to express their own opinions and feel confident to back this up with evidence or reasoned argument, the teacher's role needs to be one of encouragement. It also needs skilled questioning which leads children to respond analytically rather than jumping through hoops to come up with the correct answer! Questions should be open-ended, and should focus on a range of criteria. For example, 'Did you like that play?' limits the possible responses to 'Yes' or 'No', whereas 'What did you like about that play?' broadens the scope. 'What did you think about the sound effects they used?' focuses the reflection into a particular area, which is a necessary part of extending the children's considerations.

Glossary of theatrical terms

Children love to use new words, and in particular words which relate to theatre, film and television. At one level, there is a feeling of glamour and 'grown-upness' about such special terminology which intrigues and motivates children. But more importantly, modelling the language and encouraging them to follow your example plays an important part in extending their vocabulary, learning about language use, and increasing their knowledge and understanding of the subject.

The following 25 terms are ones which children should be able to learn and use. You will probably be familiar with many of them already, but the list is intended as a reminder to you to use them. Saying to Darren and Ben, 'OK. Stage hands, stand by to take the props on for the next scene!' can be quite an effective way of helping two such pupils to concentrate their efforts on the task in hand!

actor:	person who performs dramatic roles for an audience, term now commonly used for male and female
audition:	a test reading from a script or improvisation to help the director choose the right person for each part
auditorium:	the area of the theatre where the audience sits
blocking:	planning the moves for a scene
box office:	place from which tickets are sold
cast:	the whole set of actors in the play
costume:	specially designed clothes for the actor to wear
critic:	person who is paid to watch a play then write a review for a newspaper or magazine
dimmer board:	electrical board of dimmer switches, each of which controls a light or group of lights

director:	person who plans how the play will be performed and instructs the actors at rehearsals
down-stage:	the front of the stage nearest to the audience
dress rehearsal:	final rehearsal in costume
front of house:	the areas in front of the stage (auditorium, box office, foyer etc.)
gels:	coloured filters which are put in front of lights to create special effects
house lights:	the lights in the auditorium
props:	short for 'properties' which are items additional to scenery and costumes, which the actors need for their performance
standby!:	an instruction to members of the cast or technical team to be ready
stage hand:	assistant who helps to change scenery
stage left:	the area of the stage to the actor's left when facing the audience
stage right:	the area of the stage to the actor's right when facing the audience
strike the set:	take down the set once the play is finished
tabs:	the curtains
technical rehearsal:	penultimate rehearsal to add lighting and sound
up-stage:	the back of the stage furthest away from the audience
wings:	each side of the stage where the actors wait to come on

Chapter 6

Drama and Oracy

Our inclusion of speaking and listening as a separate profile component in our recommendations is a reflection of our conviction that these skills are of central importance to children's development.

(The Cox Report, DES 1988)

In this chapter you can read about:

- the centrality of oracy to learning
- a recent historical perspective on oracy in the primary curriculum
- the relationship between oracy and drama
- planning for range, purpose and audience
- Standard English and language study
- listening and responding.

The centrality of oracy

'Oracy' means speaking and listening, and is used in the same way that 'literacy' is used to describe reading and writing. Spoken language is central to human communication. Not only does it make meaning through words and syntactical structures, it also creates further meaning through other dynamics – tone, volume, expression, accent, speed, body language and so on. The written word can sometimes seem two-dimensional in comparison to this multi-faceted mechanism, even though the one is derived directly from the other! It is appropriate, therefore, that oracy is acknowledged by all primary teachers to be at the core of language learning.

Early language learning

Parents are their children's primary educators and an enormous amount of language learning has already taken place before each child starts formal education. Spoken language develops at a considerable rate from birth to the point at which children start school, and this prior learning is a firm foundation which schools should build on, not dismantle. To do this effectively and appropriately, teachers require a sound understanding of the complex nature of talk and the functions it serves in learning.

Vygotsky's social-psycholinguistic theory (1978) has demonstrated how young children use speech to organise their thinking, particularly when problem-solving. The running commentaries which we can observe children making as they play are clear examples of externalised thought, and there is much evidence to show that this is helpfully guiding the learning process (Berk 1994). The work of Bruner (1986) likewise explores the use of language as a tool for learning and in particular the importance of talk to assist understanding. This is easily understood when one thinks of the stream of questions which young children constantly ask as they explore and find out about their world!

There are many different theories about how children actually learn to talk, but they all have one thing in common – the vital role of interaction with others. Children do not learn to talk in isolation. They talk by hearing adults and other children modelling a wide range of examples; by experimenting with making sounds, by receiving responses to those sounds, adapting, and practising them, often through play. In other words, talk is a dynamic and interactive process.

From home to school

If such interactive processes are part and parcel of language and learning development, it is easy to see how progress might actually slow down for some children when they start school if the language environment is restrictive or alien to them (Wells 1986). To interrupt the language learning processes of the home by forcing young children into unnaturally passive roles in which they must sustain long periods of silence can prevent their natural curiosity which is such a crucial contributing factor in learning development. Furthermore, to undermine the linguistic confidence and self concept of young children by trying to modify their accent or criticising the language of the home can also inhibit and threaten their self-esteem and inhibit their motivation.

Therefore, it is vital that teachers acknowledge the learning which has already taken place in the home and what an active part the children themselves have had to play in that. The opportunities which children have had to use and explore language need to continue and develop in new directions. The cultural contexts of children's homes and the wide range of experiences which will have resulted in very different individual learning needs should also be recognised, and teachers should take an obvious interest in the life of the child beyond school.

The variation in the language of families across Britain is enormous. Not only are there cultural differences resulting from the rich ethnic diversity of our society, but also there are a multitude of dialects even within tight geographical areas. Language is laden with value systems, and carries many implicit meanings in addition to the direct meaning of words. These can often be the subject of prejudice and stereotyping which, in a classroom situation, can be very damaging. It is best therefore to start from the understanding that most children have made a significant and amazing achievement – they have learned to talk! Regardless of which dialect or mother tongue they use, they have acquired a set of sophisticated and complex skills which encompass many millions of combinations and meanings, and that has to be the starting point for the next stages of learning.

It has been argued that children whose language is closest to that of the teacher and the culture of the school are at an advantage when starting school. They are used to the linguistic structures and vocabulary, they know and use many of the social conventions, they are comfortable with the accents, and communication is therefore effective because it is a continuation of that which is familiar and in which the child has developed competence at home. On the other hand, children who bring to school a community dialect which includes relatively little Standard English, or those whose first language is not the first language of the school, are faced with a much steeper learning curve.

So how can teachers provide a learning environment where children continue to learn and think with the help of their private speech and shared talk? Clearly, it would be totally inappropriate to provide a classroom environment where children have complete freedom to pursue unlimited talk with no regard for the social rules of speaking or the needs of others and where the talk was totally unstructured and unmonitored. Oracy in the primary curriculum should be designed in such a way that children can learn *through* speaking and listening, but also learn *about* speaking and listening in order to continue developing new skills. These skills should enable them to communicate with a widening range of audiences for a widening range of purposes, and drama is an ideal way of enabling this to happen.

Oracy in the primary curriculum

As children make their way through the school system oracy sometimes becomes a diminishing part of the curriculum. Subject areas becomes increasingly compartmentalised and content-based, and passive modes of learning take over from participatory interactive learning. Pedagogically, this can be a mistake.

In 1975, the Bullock Report referred to the significance of talk during the early years of schooling as follows:

> Most nursery and infant teachers recognise that when young children are involved in some activity the talk that accompanies it becomes an important instrument for learning. Talk is a means by which they learn to work and live with one another. It enables them to gather information and build into their own experience the experience of others. (p.62, para. 5.22)

In 1988, when the Kingman Committee made its recommendations to government for reforms to the teaching of English it identified talking and listening as important parts of an integrated model for teaching the use and knowledge of language for *all* children. It also stated clearly that classrooms 'must reflect that behaviour' of speech predominance if they are to prepare children for adult life (p.42, para. 30). The same report recommended that children should learn, not only how to use talk but also how to reflect upon and analyse it in order to expand their knowledge about language.

The proposed framework for the National Curriculum for English, now referred to as The Cox Report (1988), was published later that year. The recommendation was made that the first attainment target should be called Speaking and Listening. This important component has been retained throughout all subsequent revisions to the Order for English and it is vital that teachers continue to plan for speaking and listening just as thoroughly as they do for reading and writing. Drama should be a significant part of that planning, both as a discrete area with content of its own and as a means of providing meaningful contexts for other oracy activities.

Oracy and drama

Drama is featured in the National Curriculum requirements for Speaking and Listening (Order for English) within Section 1 ('Range'), where it appears twice at each key stage. Firstly, it is stated each time in Paragraph 1a, listed as one amongst several types of talk for a purpose. Secondly, it makes a totally explicit reference to drama as follows:

Key Stage 1: Pupils should be encouraged to participate in drama activities, improvisation and performances of varying kinds, using language appropriate to a role or situation. They should be given opportunities to respond to drama they have watched, as well as that in which they have participated (para. 1d, p. 3).

Key Stage 2: Pupils should be given opportunities to participate in a wide range of drama activities, including improvisation, role-play, and the writing and performance of scripted drama. In responding to drama, they should be encouraged to evaluate their own and others' contributions (para. 1d, p. 9).

In addition to these explicit requirements, it is also obvious that drama has a valuable part to play as the mode of delivery for other oracy activities. In other words, drama facilitates a whole range of purposes for which speaking might be needed by offering roles, situations, contexts and a variety of approaches to setting these up. In drama, pupils can learn to *use* talk, and they can also learn *about* talk. Involvement and interaction are crucial components of the development of talk – drama can offer both these things!

Range

The interactive and dynamic nature of speaking and listening means that we talk for many different reasons and purposes. For example, the last hour of work, the journey home, a meal with the family and a night out with a best friend would all be likely to involve different reasons for talking – *explaining* something to a colleague, *asking* the garage attendant why the petrol pump isn't working properly, *complaining* to your partner that it's beans on toast again, and *relating* a piece of news to your friend! It is important that pupils develop an understanding of this concept of range, and are provided with opportunities to talk for a wide variety of purposes just as we do in life. Drama enables you to set up situations so that children can experience many different contexts, roles and relationships. The Order for English describes such a range of purposes in the Programmes of Study. For example:

- telling stories
- predicting outcomes
- giving reasons for actions
- describing events.

Drama has an obvious part to play in providing the mechanisms for such talk. However, when planning talk activities it is important to be guided by types of talk as well as the purpose. 'Sharing ideas' is a purpose, but for that purpose we could use various *types of talk* such as recalling, predicting, describing, suggesting, listing and so on. Planning to ensure that the children are *learning about* different types of talk and *using* different types of talk requires a sound teacher knowledge of the options available. Figure 6.1 shows two lists of talk types: **Concrete Talk**, where the talk tends to be supported by actual experience such as an event, a resource, an observation and so on; and **Abstract Talk** which is based more on thoughts and ideas. This is not a definitive list, and there is an inevitable overlapping of categories [for instance, planning might draw on recapping, sequencing and explaining]. However, they have been divided in order to help you reflect more analytically about how different types of talk require different skills and levels of knowledge.

CONCRETE TALK	ABSTRACT TALK
...based upon prior event, observation, knowledge etc.	**...based on thought, ideas, indirect experience etc.**
• retelling (story, poem, news)	• planning
• relating (messages)	• predicting
• reporting (event, results, findings)	• suggesting ideas
• reflecting (on what has happened before)	• developing ideas
• responding	• investigating
• giving instructions	• imagined stories
• explaining (choice, decision, action)	• persuading
• asking a question	• expressing opinion
• answering a question	• qualifying an argument
• listing	• expressing insights
• sequencing	
• describing	
• evaluating	
• commenting	
• justifying	
• reasoned argument	

Figure 6.1 Types of talk

When engaging in Concrete Talk, the children would usually have subject matter upon which to base their talk, whereas Abstract Talk relies more heavily on thoughts and ideas. Having said that, drama generally requires children to imagine and so they might be using Concrete Talk whilst applying imaginative and developmental skills. Arguably, this could be a further reason to justify using drama because it provides 'surrogate' subject matter for the development of abstract thought.

Figure 6.2 provides some examples of how the type of talk might lead the drama – in other words, having decided which type of talk you wish the children to engage in, a drama activity can be designed in order to provide that opportunity.

TALK TYPE	
• reporting	KS1 – school role-play, teacher reporting on pupils' performance
	KS2 – role-play in pairs, reporting a burgulary in a shopping centre
• explaining	KS1 – explaining to Goldilocks why she was rude to invade the three bears' house
	KS2 – in role as historical character, explaining a trade or event
• asking questions	KS1 – travel agents' role-play area/taking bookings
	KS2 – role-play interviews in pairs
• predicting	KS1 – spontaneous improvisation, exploring a secret castle, predicting what they might find
	KS2 – group presentation of a famous scientific discovery
• investigating	KS1 – following clues (which you have written and hidden) in the home corner
	KS2 – documentary on an investigation into bullying
• expressing opinion	KS1 – about a play they have been to see at the theatre
	KS2 – role-play of two opposing politicians talking about banning parking in cities

Figure 6.2 Talk types in drama contexts

Audience

Talk is pointless unless we have something to talk about and someone to talk to! We talk differently according to our audience – speaking more formally to some than others. Even those we know well can unknowingly demand different styles, for example speaking to a parent, a sibling and a friend might result in different tone and vocabulary, speaking to a friend of one gender might be different to speaking to a friend of the other gender, and so on. The Order for English makes specific reference to audience in the attainment target for speaking and listening, requiring children to identify the needs of different audiences and speak in ways which address those needs.

Providing audiences helps to motivate the children because it gives the activity a purpose and a focus. The audience in question might be 'real', for example other groups, the whole class, other classes, parents, senior citizens and so on. On the other hand, drama can also provide any other audience you wish by putting the children in role. In other words, the drama can provide 'pretend audiences' as well as 'pretend speakers'!

Audience in role

Imagine that you want children to explain the things they do at school, paying attention to describing carefully and also justifying why. Ask them to plan a presentation in groups, imagining that they are the teachers of a school (similar or very different to their own). The headteacher has invited all the new parents to a meeting at the start of the school year to give them information about the school. As each group 'performs' their prepared presentation in role, the rest of the children will also be in role as the visiting parents. They will listen critically so that they can ask questions (as parents). This not only serves the purpose of focusing the minds of the presenters on their target audience but also creates an added dimension to the process of listening – a more participatory involvement than simply hearing passively. The 'audience in role' approach also offers the chance for peer evaluation and giving feedback to each other about how they spoke and how they listened. Questions such as:

'How did the teachers use their voices when they were explaining?'

'Did they answer the questions clearly?'

can add useful teaching opportunities about the use of language.

The list in Figure 6.3 shows some other examples of how the children could provide specific audiences in role.

ACTIVITY	AUDIENCE ROLE
Home corner role-play	Teacher as neighbour calling in for cup of tea
Pair police interviews	Pupil in role as police requiring a clear description
Documentary programme	Class as TV critics
Teacher operating hand puppets	Pupils asking the puppets questions
Group story performance	Other groups guessing the moral of the story
Explaining electricity	People from Tudor times
Describing an earthquake	News reporters at a press conference
Giving instructions about a picnic event	Teddy bears

Figure 6.3 Creating audiences through drama

Audiences can come in different sizes, and it is worth referring to Chapter 4 to see how children can be grouped in different ways for different purposes relating to the 'audience in role' approach.

Listening and responding

Listening is a vital part of oracy, and there are clear expectations within the National Curriculum about how children should use and develop their listening skills. However, listening is difficult to monitor, because it is not as observable as we sometimes assume. The well-worn expectation, 'I want you to listen quietly!' belies the true complexity of listening skills. Children might be still and quiet, but how can you know that they are listening. They might be miles away, dreaming about a forthcoming birthday party! It can be helpful to ask yourself what you expect from their listening? There are two main outcomes which should be required from listening: understanding and response, and these two are closely linked.

Understanding leads to extension or adaptation of knowledge and concepts. If children listen with understanding, they are more likely to remember what they have heard. In turn, they can respond, which helps them to assimilate further and use that knowledge in transferrable ways. Response comes in many shapes and sizes: following instructions, answering questions, retelling, disagreeing, making relevant comment and so on.

In order to assess children's listening skills, you need to be clear about the expected outcomes which you believe provide evidence of understanding and/or response. This is discussed in more detail in Chapter 10, but here are some questions which you might ask during drama activities to ascertain the quality of the listening:

- *Police interview:* are they asking questions which build on the evidence given?
- *Public debate:* are they using the arguments of others to make a case against the opposition?

- *Watching a group performance:* can they compare and contrast two types of talk?
- *Role-play corner:* can they follow three separate instructions in sequence?

When setting up listening activities, the quality of the listening will depend to a great extent on the interesting nature of the talk. It is only human for all of us to switch off when we are bored! This is another reason why drama can be a useful tool – it can bring the activity 'alive', adding to it a compelling desire to listen. However, you also need to make it clear to the children that you have expectations of their listening, e.g. 'As we continue with the public meeting I am going to make notes on how you use other people's arguments to build up your own points.' 'As we make our journey together across the desert island, I am going to give you clues about who I am, which I will ask you to remember at the end when we get back to the classroom.'

Watching the drama of others, whether it be other groups in the class or a professional performance, enables children to create new knowledge and theorise about that knowledge. Discussing, analysing and interpreting will help children with the process of assimilating the experience.

Standard English and language study

Language is complex and fascinating to study! It is constantly changing, a living, breathing, developing animal! Standard English is only one of many forms of language construction or dialects. It is the central 'rule book' form as taught to speakers of other languages and is necessary for common communication in the world of business, media, politics and international affairs etc. – in other words, situations where a commonly-agreed format is necessary to enable all participants to understand each other clearly. This does not mean that other dialects are 'inferior', they are simply different. Regional dialects are community-based, specific to particular geographic areas, and therefore do not necessarily have all the common features required for wider communication. However, the rich variation of sounds, structures and vocabulary which can be found around Britain are interesting and colourful, and should be seen as part of our cultural heritage rather than something which should be homogenised into one single form.

Certain linguistic features can also be specific to age groups, for example some 'teenage words and phrases' transcend all geographical divisions, and yet are rarely used by other generations! To further complicate matters, this changes from decade to decade. The vocabulary of teenagers in the 60s (e.g. 'groovy', 'fab', and 'flower power') was very different from that of young people today (e.g. 'cool', 'well bad', and 'sorted')! The adaptations of words and the development of new words, not just by teenagers, are processes which have happened all the way through history. One only has to compare texts from Chaucer, Shakespeare and Austen to see examples of this, along with all the Eurospeak and information technology vocabulary which has flooded the English language during the 90s. Language changes, grows, and adapts, and this can be an interesting subject to explore with children as a means of teaching them to be informed users.

Language also has powerful social connotations of power, status and worth. Stereotyping according to accent or dialect is still, sadly, a common feature of British society. As teachers we should be extremely careful not to alienate children, or threaten their self-esteem by dismantling the language which is part of their identity. Dialects are an important part of the majority of children's lives because they have been central to their language and learning prior to starting school, and continue to be central to their lives at home and in their communities alongside the language of the school.

Nevertheless, if children are to have equal opportunities in a society where different dialects, including Standard English, are required for different purposes and audiences, then it is vital that we provide them with the multilingual skills to switch from one to another, and the knowledge of when and why it is appropriate to do so. Using linguistic variation through drama can make it possible to present many different language scenarios in order to motivate children to learn about language whilst at the same time developing their user skills in a range of situations. Examples of such activities might include:

- writing dialect poems and raps for performance
- looking at and performing dialect from stories and poems
- recording radio adverts with different accents
- using regional words in drama (e.g. bread roll, bap, batch, cob, flour cake etc.)
- transcribing dialect from soap operas into Standard English and performing both versions
- translation of parts of the drama by speakers of other languages
- writing alternative scripts of talk for different purposes
- comparing the grammar of spoken forms arising from improvisations with written forms (script versus a report of the scene)
- discussing the differences between boys' talk and girls' talk during a class improvisation where the pupils change gender roles
- improvising formal situations such as job interviews.

Providing models for talk

Just as children's early language development relies upon exposure to and interaction with other people speaking, so do they need to hear different examples of speech if they are to learn a range of approaches to language. Different types of talk require different constructions and vocabulary, for example, predicting normally uses the future tense whereas reporting uses the past. If children are going to learn to use features of Standard English for particular purposes, they need to hear good examples upon which they can model their own attempts. Modelling can be provided by tapes, video, visitors, and most of all by you. However, an approach which demonstrates, drills, and criticises is not going to be as effective as following the natural processes of hearing, using and re-hearing. Drama enables children to use the language, and interact with you in role while you model the language you are teaching. Here are some examples:

- *Planning a camping trip: use of future tense:* 'What are we going to take with us... I am going to take a warm sleeping bag. What are you going to take, Dean?'
- *Reporting what happened during a midnight visit to Santa's workshop:* use of past tense: So what happened next, Leanne? Oh, you found a pile of empty sacks. I wonder why they were empty? What did you find, Carl? You found a kettle which was still warm? What did you think about that?'
- *Interview with headteacher about an incident: use of conjunctions:* 'So you threw the ball outside the gates because you were cross with Jason. Did you tell anyone before you climbed over the wall?'

You will notice from these examples that modelling includes repeating back to the child the correct version, so that they are hearing it more than once as well as saying it themselves.

Extending vocabulary

If children are provided with situations which require new vocabulary they will also need preparation and resources to help them access that vocabulary as well as building on the models you provide in your own language. This might come from a range of places such as:

- introductory explanations
- hearing texts read aloud
- researching from texts
- tapes and videos
- labels on the wall
- game cards.

The drama can be constructed in ways which will require the children to use the vocabulary, for example words such as 'conflict', 'debate', 'decision' and 'finalise' could be focus words used during a public meeting. Or when reporting an event, rather than stringing together their ideas with 'and then' children could be encouraged to use other conjunctions by using conjunction cue cards (large flash cards each with a conjunction on them: after/since/whenever/although/because/except that, etc). Each time they use a card they score a point, so the drama in this context is more of a language game.

Although it may not always be appropriate to 'interrupt' the drama, you should take every opportunity you can to make explicit the points you are aiming to teach. This is usually done most successfully by acknowledgement and praise.

Speaking clearly and confidently

Clarity is something which can be modelled for children, but which they also need to practise. Clarity requires appropriate speed and volume. It also requires expression which helps the meaning, and logical organisation where a sequence of ideas is being expressed. Clarity is about successfully 'reaching' your audience.

There is a world of difference between forcing children to alter their natural speech as 'themselves' and asking them to do this in role. Working in role can assist learning in the following ways:

- it protects self-esteem by de-personalising a process which is, in reality, an extremely personal and sensitive part of a child's self perception
- it provides enjoyable reasons for speaking 'differently'
- it offers the disguise or mask of someone different in which to experiment
- it enables you to correct the 'character' rather than the child
- it helps children to understand diversity as opposed to one 'wrong way' of speaking and one 'correct way' of speaking
- it provides a context for repetition, practice and preparation.

Children who lack confidence in their own speech can often be nurtured by working in role. As they become more confident with this, they can gradually transfer skills such as presenting, explaining, debating and so on to speaking activities which relate to their own personal work.

Oracy, drama and the literacy hour

During your daily hour of literacy, the National Literacy Strategy framework (NLS) requires you to use a 'wide range of teaching strategies' (DfEE 1998). It also states quite clearly that the work carried out during this time should contain 'high quality oral work', 'discussing and arguing', 'listening and responding'. Modelling and scaffolding are also crucial features of the teaching strategies listed, and children are expected to work in ways which are 'interactive', 'well paced' and 'ambitious'. Drama is a valid tool to use during the literacy hour, and although reading and writing are at the heart of the objectives for this teaching time, it is important to remember that, where oracy skills are an integral part of the process, the learning is deeper and longer-lasting. With judicious and well-planned construction, drama can help you construct the oral elements of literacy learning because it enables you to:

- model language in role
- provide opportunities for children to explore and discuss language in role
- use texts as starting points for exploration
- link reading and writing in meaningful contexts
- play language games for repetition and consolidation
- define changes of pace and focus during the hour (e.g. teacher in role/questions/ writing follow-up/performance/evaluation and feedback).

There is a clear message in the NLS that 'pupils must be working on texts' during the hour. However, this should not mean labouring through dry de-contextualised exercises for six consecutive years! Children will learn best about literacy at word, sentence and text level only if they *talk* about and *use* those texts.

Summary

The growth of a child's confidence will depend to a very large extent upon your attitudes and the ethos you create in your classroom. An oracy environment which is supportive, active and interesting is going to be more effective than one which is critical, didactic and restrictive. Modelling and praise are powerful tools, as we see when babies imitate sounds and then repeat them in response to the attention poured upon them for doing so! Expectations should be clear and realistic. Progression should be developmental and satisfying. Drama enables all these things to happen, and should constitute a significant part of every school's schemes of work for speaking and listening.

Chapter 7

Drama and Reading

Drama techniques play an important role within and beyond the Literacy Hour as a means of responding to a text. (The National Literacy Strategy. Module 5: Teachers' Notes DfEE 1998b)

In this chapter you can read about:

- the complexity of reading
- how drama can assist the reading processes
- a model of interaction between drama and reading
- different levels of textual exploration
- categories and sources of texts
- reading interrogation strategies
- the role of literature in drama.

Introduction

The reason that we read is to access meaning for an infinite number of purposes! The enjoyment and appreciation of literature is one obvious example of why we read, but we also read in other ways and for other purposes. For example, we read a shopping list as a reminder, we read a poster to find out details of an event, we read a contract to check what we are signing, we read directions to find our way to a venue, and so the list goes on. This requires us to:

- locate and select appropriate texts
- interact with texts
- respond to texts.

Such processes are intellectually dynamic and interrogatory – it is not always easy to learn how to use them by sitting passively with a text provided by someone else. Drama is an ideal way of providing situations in which children can interact with texts and in doing so become proactive and responsive readers. This chapter helps you to understand how you might plan for this to happen in your classroom, but first let us take a closer look at other things which also need to be addressed in the teaching of reading.

The complexity of reading

Reading is a complex task involving different strategies which operate together at different levels to create meaning from text. To read a text we need to be able to:

- recognise the shapes of the letters and words (graphemic knowledge)
- relate these to the sounds they make (phonemic knowledge)

- interpret the ways in which the words are organised to make meaning from the grammar (syntactic knowledge)
- interpret the words and context into meaning (semantic knowledge).

(These four strategies are similarly represented as 'Searchlights' in the NLS Teaching Framework (DfEE 1998a) because they are said to 'shed light on the text'.)

Although there may appear to be a sort of hierarchical progression to these four strategies, in reality they operate simultaneously. However, children who are just starting to read are having to direct more of their efforts into decoding skills, which is why it is so important to provide early readers with books at the right level of difficulty. Research shows that where children are struggling with a text which is too far beyond their grapho-phonemic knowledge, they are so busy focusing in on the letters and sounds that they are not accessing meaning (Clay 1979; Stanovich 1980). This is usually why, when we listen to children reading in this laborious way, they are usually unable to answer questions about the story very accurately when they reach the end. As they develop into more fluent readers, the first two strategies become more automatic, and the proportion of attention on meaning and responding increases.

It is also important to remember that decoding and understanding texts is only part of the picture. The raison d'être of reading is response. Responding to texts can mean many different things, from reading that shopping list to engaging in a fierce debate about the sentimentality (or not!) of Heathcliff in *Wuthering Heights*. In other words, we do not learn to read because it is a statutory hurdle, but we learn to read because it is a tool that we shall use all our lives for a multitude of purposes. If children are going to develop an understanding of how different modes of response are required by different text situations they will need to interact with texts in ways which will illicit a range of responses.

There is much research to show that interest in and attitudes towards reading tend to decline at Key Stage 2 (OFSTED 1996). There are many reasons for this, and many solutions. The systematic approach of the NLS will do much to broaden the scope of how reading continues to be taught at Key Stage 2 as the misconception that teaching reading is the responsibility only of infant teachers is gradually outlawed. Drama can also do much to address this problem with older readers if it offers them models of reading, and categories of texts in addition to literature, which help them to perceive themselves as readers in the adult world. A model to illustrate this was first published in *Reading On! Developing Reading at Key Stage 2*, eds. Reid and Bentley 1996, (Chapter 4, 'Teaching Reading Through Drama', Clipson-Boyles). The description and diagram of the model are reproduced in the next section with the kind permission of Scholastic Ltd.

A model of interaction between drama and reading

The National Curriculum requirements for reading are of an active rather than a passive nature. Children are required to respond and relate to a wide variety of texts. They need to read for a range of purposes, and employ different reading skills at different times. They are required to develop a knowledge of literature along with the confidence to express their own views. They need to be efficient and selective in the retrieval of information from different sources. Such requirements demand interactive models of learning, and drama is the ideal medium for many activities which will extend and develop pupils as readers.

The model presented here demonstrates a theory of the relationship between drama and reading which is designed to promote what has been called 'The Evolution of the Reader'.

The 'Evolution of the Reader' represents an organic and wholesome growth of the developmental processes of four main operations of reading: graphemic/phonemic, syntactic, semantic and responsive. These four operations of reading develop simultaneously, although not necessarily at the same pace. At Key Stage 2, graphemic/phonemic awareness and syntactic competence are, for the

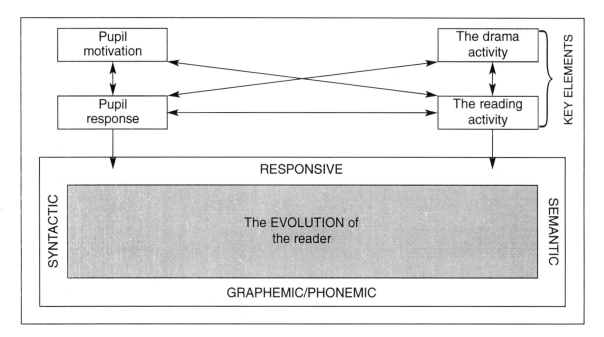

Figure 7.1 A model of interaction between drama and reading

majority of pupils, well established, while semantic operations cannot always be assumed. The responsive capabilities of older readers will have been developed to a range of levels, but will now be ripe for a more rapid rate of growth. The evolutionary process is the unfolding of the reader into an increasingly complex creature and takes place from babyhood to adulthood.

The model illustrates how drama can be a significant contributing factor to the evolutionary process for junior readers. It illustrates four interrelated elements which are significant to the process and have been named the 'Key Elements'. These are:

- the reading activity, i.e. the text and purpose, for example scanning a newspaper for information
- pupil response, i.e. consequence of reading, for example following an instruction, empathising
- pupil motivation, i.e. the pupil's level of willingness or enthusiasm
- the drama activity, i.e. the context and vehicle for the reading

The reading activity

It is clear to most teachers that children will not evolve as readers unless they read! As illustrated by the model, experience of reading is contributing directly to the evolutionary process. This experience will provide opportunities to learn and practise the different operations listed earlier (included in the 'Evolution' box in the diagram). However, at junior level, there is a considerable shift towards independent reading and this can sometimes mean that the reader is left to cope alone without the necessary skills to get the best out of the activity. The reading might take place without any increase in the level of sophistication. In many cases, the reading does not take place because the child has lost interest or simply can't be bothered.

The pupil response

The response operation has been separated out for the purposes of the model because it is considered to be the most appropriate aspect of reading to be developed through drama. Pupil response is considered to be the least likely to evolve directly from independent reading activities.

Drama addresses the socially interactive nature of response, facilitating discussion, exploration and debate. This discrete inclusion of reader response in the model highlights the fact that it is a major area for development, although as texts are read, other skills are sometimes addressed.

Pupil motivation

Lack of motivation to read is identified regularly by teachers as a significant problem with some older primary school children. This sometimes manifests itself in the form of poor knowledge of authors, reluctance to try something new, or professed boredom with books. If teachers are to continue assisting the evolutionary process, they need to ensure that their children are motivated to read.

The drama activity

In sharp contrast, drama is usually extremely popular with most children – lessons are characterised by enthusiasm, energy and commitment. Such positive attitudes to this type of learning can be harnessed to deliver an exciting and productive approach to reading development.

The value of drama in reading

You will, by now, be familiar with the principles of experiential learning through drama and the range of approaches which are available to you. You will also recognise that New Wave Drama embraces such learning in harmony with language work, cross curricular language skills and theatre arts, each integrating with the other or not, according to the aims of the activity. All these elements offer contexts for reading activities. Here are some examples.

Props which will be used in role-play: Newspapers, telephone directories, recipe books in the role-play corner will be used by children in play and extend their concepts of print and awareness of purposes for reading. Older children can be given texts to actually read during improvisation, such as a letter to stimulate response, newspaper article to provide information for a police interview and so on.

Exploring storyline: Re-enactment of stories in their own language can provide an enjoyable reason for shared reading beforehand.

Exploring beyond the storyline: Additional parts of the story, alternative endings, expanding implicit parts of the story, can be played out during improvisation, and also worked into small-scale performance.

Understanding character motivation: Taking sections of story to explore why characters acted in certain ways, or improvising characters' thoughts can lead to useful analysis, and train children into thinking more deeply about text and sub-text.

Sequencing and performing story: Giving story sections to children and asking them to sequence the sections and to present their work to others is a good reading-for-meaning task. Exploring the effects of changing the sequence can provide opportunities for further analysis and discussion about story structure.

Researching for the drama: Use of information books can provide material for drama. For instance, creating tableaux or plays about the Ancient Greeks, to share with the rest of the class. Further discussion about the parts which were fact and those which were fiction offers scope for justification and accountability by giving references in answer to questioning by the others after their presentation.

Research arising from the drama: Sometimes, themes or issues will emerge during the drama that will benefit from further research afterwards, particularly in combination with follow-up writing activities.

Word games: Charades which have to include new vocabulary can involve reading first in order to select those words.

Information needed for script writing: Script writing might be in response to prior improvisation which has prompted further research, or may require reading in order to search for ideas.

Preparation for simulation: Sometimes, a simulation can be planned and prepared by the children rather than by you. This will require research, for example, how is a newsroom set out? Who works there? What will be on their desks? What sort of equipment do you find in offices?

Starting points for presentations: Presentation might mean puppet show, radio interview, tableaux sequence etc. The reading can be a starting point for this, e.g. a story reported in a newspaper, a letter.

Models for writing in role: The National Curriculum and the NLS state repeatedly that children should be shown models of good practice in writing. If we expect children to produce a poster, they need to see lots of different examples of posters and discuss the features. Writing in role is also enhanced by the provision of 'real' texts because it helps the children to pretend.

You may have noticed, as you read these examples, that the reading can connect with the drama at different times;

Before the drama: e.g. as preparation or stimulus
During the drama: e.g. as prop for role-play, for reading aloud, as instruction
After the drama: e.g. follow up inquiry, reading responses, further information

These alternative positionings will affect the reading interrogation strategies, because the purpose will be different each time. This is a good argument for varying the positioning of the reading when planning drama activities.

Another important area of consideration has to be the range of texts which you provide for these activities. How can you provide a really exciting range of texts, and how do you go about equipping your classroom with such vast quantities of reading materials? How do you contextualise the activities for the children, and why is it so necessary to go to all this trouble?

Categories of texts and interrogation strategies

If children are going to develop a response repertoire and become proactive independent readers they need to understand that in our society there is a vast range of things to read! This principle of 'range' is a central thread running through the National Curriculum requirements and NLS guidelines for the teaching of English. Children should be provided with opportunities to speak and write for a range of purposes, in a range of styles, and for a range of audiences. Likewise, with reading, teachers are expected to provide children with a range of genres, and texts within those genres. The NLS Teaching Framework (DfEE 1998) provides a comprehensive and systematic approach to teaching reading and writing at word, sentence and text levels, and offers guidance on text range by recommending different genres of fiction, poetry and non fiction for each term of primary schooling. This not only ensures that there is good coverage of genres for every child but also helps teachers to plan activities which combine the systematic teaching of strategies within a range of literary contexts. Children need to use and develop reading and writing through meaningful activities which relate to 'real' texts rather than practising language exercises in a dissociated vacuum. Drama is an invaluable teaching approach with which you can help children to learn effectively in this way.

Providing a variety of texts enables children to adopt different approaches to reading according to

	LITERATURE	NON FICTION	REFERENCE	LEISURE TEXTS	COMMERCIAL TEXTS	DOCUMENTS
EXAMPLES	• children's own writing • novels • picture books • plays • poetry • short stories	• biographies • coffee table books • hobbies/interests • manuals • recipes/DIY • text books	• atlases • databases • dictionaries • directories • encyclopaedias • internet • *time-tables*	• cartoon books • comics • joke books • magazines • newspapers • football programmes • *TV guides*	• advertisements • catalogues • flyers • labels • leaflets • posters • *price lists*	• contracts • faxes • forms • letters • memos • minutes • *reports*
SOME FUNCTIONS OF THE DRAMA	• explore character • develop storyline • perform • sequencing	• use for research • use in role-play • explore beyond a picture • answer questions after drama	• reference in role-play • word games • seek information for script writing • information for simulation	• props for characters • character information • story starting points • making news programmes	• business role play • props and scenery • starting point for improvisation • models for writing in role	• office role-play • writing in role • artefacts as stimulus for improvisation • follow-up writing

Figure 7.2 Categories of text with drama examples

the type of text and the purpose. Texts other than fiction demand a wide range of reading interrogation strategies, sometimes even within the same booklet or magazine. For example a football programme guide might be read by comparing the players on each team before a match. This would involve scanning, focusing in, cross-referencing from one to another to compare, and responding by assessing the chances of each team based on the selection. On the other hand, in another section of the same programme, a feature article on the captain would require reading through from beginning to end.

Encountering different categories of texts helps to:

- broaden children's concepts of textual diversity
- expand their perceptions of themselves as readers
- increase their repertoire of reading interrogation strategies
- stimulate their interest in reading.

The NLS guidance of fiction, poetry and non-fiction provides very useful guidance to ensure that a broad range is covered during the six primary years and that literacy teaching links directly to the texts. It can also be helpful to think of texts across categories as well as within genres when planning to use drama to help children interact with and respond to texts. A model of six categories is presented here with some examples of how the drama might link into each category. This is not a definitive categorisation, and there are obvious areas of overlap where certain texts might fit into more than one category, but the model is a useful way to identify potential texts, and use their associated sources as a starting point for drama (e.g. contracts = employment scenario).

Obtaining free resources

Good quality resources are crucial to good quality teaching, but we all know that high costs can be involved in the purchase of books. However, collecting free reading materials is also a possibility, and this can bring additional bonuses, such as:

- you can collect sets (e.g. six theme park leaflets)
- you can involve business and commercial partners in education (e.g. local shops or tourist information)
- you are involving parents and helping them to understand the breadth of the reading repertoire for their child (i.e. 'the reading book' is not the only thing which is there to be read)
- children enjoy the feeling of using 'real world' texts and pretending to be adults
- it provides variety, which is the spice of learning as well as life!

In some shops you can help yourself to leaflets, flyers and brochures, in some you will have to ask. It is also worth remembering that used items can also be useful and free, e.g. newspapers, TV guides, football programmes, theatre posters, comics etc. Most parents, neighbours, friends and relatives are usually only too happy to save these for you – better to re-use things for a worthwhile cause than throw them away!

Reading interrogation strategies

Having discussed the range of purposes and the variety of texts which children need to encounter, let us now think about the range of strategies which they might use to extract information when reading.

Here are some examples of different reading interrogation strategies (RIS) being used during drama. The six text categories are represented, one in each example.

(KS1) EXAMPLE 1	**_Justifying Decisions_**
TEXT:	*Would You Rather...*, John Burningham (1978)
CATEGORY:	Literature
ACTIVITY:	Improvisations of some of the activities in the book, then choosing from the alternatives offered ('Would you rather have...supper in a castle, breakfast in a balloon, or tea on the river?')
RIS:	Reading for meaning, comparing, decision making, justifying decisions

(KS2) EXAMPLE 2	**_Radio programme on Karate_**
TEXT:	Selection of information books about karate
CATEGORY:	Non fiction/Leisure texts/Commercial texts
ACTIVITY:	Research from texts to write and present a radio programme 'Karate Through the Keyhole: a 5 minute tour!' (Other hobbies could also be used)
RIS:	Reading for information, comparing, selecting, sequencing and communicating the information in a new form

(KS1) EXAMPLE 3	**_Fixing the Washing Machine_**
TEXT:	Yellow Pages/Report Forms/Instruction Leaflets
CATEGORY:	Reference
ACTIVITY:	After explanation of Yellow Pages and washing machine instruction leaflet, provide overalls, tools, report forms. Role-play/Practice/Show
RIS:	Alphabetical sequence/reading for information

(KS2) EXAMPLE 4	**_Footballer Interview_**
TEXT:	Football magazine
CATEGORY:	Leisure texts
ACTIVITY:	Give them a star interview to read and ask them to establish what sort of things are asked. Improvise interviews, trying to remember the information, OR with 'new' stars, inventing different information which can then be written into a new article.
RIS:	Reading for information/analysis of sections

(KS1) EXAMPLE 5	**_Cafe Role-play_**
TEXT:	Selection of menus
CATEGORY:	Commercial texts
ACTIVITY:	Show and discuss menus. Groups of four pretend to be new cafe owners planning the opening of a new cafe. Design posters and menus (in role).
RIS:	Reading for information/seeking spellings/learning format

(KS2) EXAMPLE 6	**_Re-designing Parkland_**
TEXT:	Report (created by you) about the proposed redesign of the local park.
CATEGORY:	Documents
ACTIVITY:	Put children in role as local community action group. In role as councillor, give each group a copy of the report to discuss. Ask for list of responses, to be presented to council meeting.
RIS:	Reading for information/analysis of separate points/responding to each point

The role of literature in drama

We have been looking, so far, at how drama can 'serve' the reading process. It is also worthwhile considering how literature can actually feed into the drama. Plays were written to be performed, and there are many playwrights, the Bard included, who would probably turn in their graves if they could see the tortured way in which pupils in some secondary schools are asked dissect and interpret their texts without even so much as five minutes action during the hour's lesson! (The principles of flexible time, pick-and-mixing methods, and the learning benefits of experiential approaches is as true for Key Stage 3, GCSE and A Level learners as it is for primary children!)

Reading-scheme plays

One of the positive responses to the National Curriculum was that publishers started to produce more plays for children, as part of, or supplements to, their reading schemes. Here are some good examples:

- Oxford Reading Tree Play-scripts   (OUP)
- Playhouse   (Nelson)
- Plays for New Readers   (Longman)
- Plays for Infants: Traditional Tales   (Ginn)
- Reading 2000 Play-scripts   (Longman)
- Storychest Plays   (Kingscourt)
- Sunshine Plays   (Heinemann)
- Whodunnits.   (Collins)

Teachers seem to agree unanimously that children love reading plays. Reading plays in groups is beneficial to young children's reading development because:

- the group situation is fun
- reading together provides inbuilt support
- the turn-taking breaks the reading into 'bite-size chunks'
- the children are encouraged to read ahead so they are ready for their next turn
- children rarely wander off-task because they have to be ready to read at different points
- the implicit purpose is to create meaning
- interpreting stage directions (when they are included) offers a good context for reading for meaning and following instruction
- dramatising the play gives additional support to accessing the meaning
- dramatising the play encourages reading with expression
- dramatising the play encourages fluent reading
- re-reading is quite appropriate, and offers children a valid reason to aim for a higher standard without feeling they are failing.

Plays for older children

In addition to reading-scheme books, older readers enjoy working with scripts from real plays. This adds the following benefits to those in the previous list:

- it helps to broaden their knowledge of literature
- it also helps them to start learning about famous playwrights
- they can start to make links with real theatre
- they can compare styles of writing
- they can look at plays historically
- there are more detailed stage directions demanding more interpretation.

Most large public libraries have drama sections from which you can borrow sets of play scripts for extended periods. It is advisable to read through the plays yourself first if you don't know them. Plays offer a range of genres – thrillers, musicals, classics, historical, fringe, pantomime, children's plays and so on. It is unlikely that you would ever wish children to read a play in its entirety, although the option to read on independently is an excellent way of extending more able readers. Some extracts can offer a self-contained story within a scene.

You may wish to use an extract as a stimulus for improvising then writing an alternative ending or beginning. A good example of this is the dramatic final scene in Brecht's *Caucasian Chalk Circle* (published by Penguin 1966). Grusha and Natella have come to court so that the judge, Azdak, can decide which is the real mother of the young child. He resolves the conflict, in his wisdom, by drawing a chalk circle and placing the child in the centre. He instructs the two women to each take one of the child's arms and pull. Whoever pulls the child out of the circle is to keep him. Each time, Grusha lets go of the child's arm for fear of hurting him, and Azdak knows that she is indeed the true mother. This scene is critically tense, and children enjoy building up the dramatic moments. Working out their own stories about how this situation emerged can result in some wonderful written work and further drama! Avid readers nearly always want to read the missing parts of the play afterwards!

The place of Shakespeare in the primary school

Many secondary school pupils struggle with Shakespeare. (Many adults also struggle with Shakespeare! You might be one of them...If you are, read on!) It is a sad reality that Shakespeare's plays are regarded by many as unattainable for them. An academic and somewhat elitist barrier exists which prevents many people from believing that these plays have any part to play in their lives. This is probably due to the endless analysis, dissection, debate, controversy and intellectual possession which has taken over ownership of the plays. Shakespeare himself would not be happy with this state of affairs! His plays were written to be performed and enjoyed by all people, and in his day they were acted out in the streets of towns and village squares to all and sundry, and they were extremely popular.

If children encounter some of Shakespeare's stories in primary school, they are more likely to approach their studies later with confidence and a better understanding. Perhaps more importantly, they will feel 'ownership' of this part of our heritage and continue to visit theatres to see his plays for the rest of their lives.

Shakespeare in the primary school should be approached initially through story. The stories are wonderful, and children will enjoy hearing you tell them, either in your own words or from one of the many splendid abridged versions, for example:

- *Shakespeare's Stories*, by Leon Garfield (Gollancz 1985)
- *Shakespeare. The Animated Tales*, by Leon Garfield (Heinemann 1992)
- *Favourite Tales from Shakespeare*, by B. Miles (Hamlyn 1986).

Activities might include:

- telling a spooky story (*Macbeth*) in a darkened room using a torch
- making puppets to play out parts of the story
- improvise short sections
- thematic mobiles (e.g. *Macbeth* daggers and witches!)
- abstract art work of themes and moods
- making model play sets
- shortened versions of the play for assembly
- playing with parts of language
- cartoon strips
- creating backing sound effects (e.g. to 'Hubble, bubble...').

'Doing Shakespeare' does not and should not mean taking on a whole play in its original entirety. Short sections can be very productive, and certainly offer enough scope for activities (e.g. the Pyramus and Thisbe play within *A Midsummer Night's Dream*). The BBC animated videos are also a very useful resource to support other work.

All these suggestions have been successfully tried and tested with eight to eleven year olds. Their enthusiasm was immense, and the real thrill was to meet one of them six years later and hear him say, 'I'm the best at Shakespeare in my set! I loved it when we did *The Dream* in your class!' (He was one of the boys seen chasing round the playground when he was eight yelling 'Away, ye vile canker blossoms'!)

Chapter 8

Drama and Writing

Thinking of a story to act out in the role-play corner is the very well-spring of creative writing as indicated.
(Chris Heald 1993)

In this chapter you can read about:

- providing opportunities for children to write for a range of purposes and audiences
- how drama can help you to provide meaningful contexts for writing
- how writing skills can be supported by drama at different developmental stages
- the links between drama and other genres
- the importance of responding to children's writing
- useful resources for drama and writing.

Writing in the primary school

At one time, the most common writing task for primary school pupils was so-called 'one-shot' writing. From the children's point of view the main purpose of the writing was so that it could be marked, and therefore the only perceived reader was the teacher. The genre would usually be story (narrative) – a title would be given, the story written in one complete draft, collected, marked and given back later in the week. However, since the 1980s, it has been recognised that this approach to writing is limited in terms of teaching children to understand and use writing in more complex and sophisticated ways.

Professional writers tend not to complete a final copy at first sitting! The planning, writing, editing, proof-reading, re-drafting and final copy are all valuable parts of the writing process, involving different reading and writing skills. Of course, not all of these stages are needed for every piece of writing, and learning when and when not to employ them is part of understanding the writing process. It is also part of knowing that there is a wide variety of reasons for writing, and many formats in which to write.

Another development in the last 20 years has been a move towards broadening the variety of genres in which children are required to write. In the real world, adults do not just write stories. (Indeed, many adults do not write stories at all!) If you stop to think about how many writing activities you have engaged in during the last week, you will see that you have probably applied your writing skills in a whole range of ways – filling in forms, shopping lists, letters, notes, messages on birthday cards, email, resource cards for school, report forms and so on. These written forms were probably intended for different readers – your partner, a window company, the Inland Revenue and so on. The Programme of Study for Writing in the National Curriculum Order for English places great emphasis on this notion of range. It focuses particularly on four things:

- writing for a range of purposes (e.g. to instruct, amuse, remind etc.)
- writing in a range of structures (e.g. note form, list, poem etc.)
- writing for a range of readers (e.g. other children, TV producers, politicians etc.)
- responding to a range of stimuli (e.g. different texts, music, drama etc.).

It is within this environment of range that key skills should be taught. Spelling, handwriting, punctuation, grammar and authorship are the tools of writing, but if children are taught to use these tools in meaningless and detached ways, they are not going to make the conceptual connections between skills and function. Writing needs to be enjoyable and purposeful if children are going to develop into motivated and independent writers. Providing variety will help them to learn about writing and will also maintain their interest!

When they start school, most children already have a considerable amount of implicit knowledge about the writing process. Goodman (1990) has identified a comprehensive list of purposes for which children between the ages of two and six years have written spontaneously. These illustrate clearly that children imitate what they see around them in their play, and that this is a significant part of their learning. We live in a world which is immersed in print – food packets, bill posters, text on television, post, newspapers, magazines, leaflets and so on, all in addition to the print in books. Children can learn from these that:

- print carries messages and meaning
- those messages can be spoken out loud
- print is represented by symbols
- print is different from pictures.

In school, we set about the business of making children's knowledge explicit – in other words, helping them to become aware of what they know so that new knowledge can be built on those foundations. We should never underestimate the importance of early concepts about print, because to teach without them is like building a house on sand…As their knowledge and experiences of print grow, young children develop new understandings such as directionality, the differences between letters and words, letter formation, how letter sounds relate to shapes, and so the list goes on. Learning to write is developmental, so to force children into formal and meaningless exercises with no regard for current levels of conceptual understanding can waste time and lead to frustration and even fear of writing.

How drama can help children to write

Teachers have become highly skilled in formulating writing activities which give children 'real reasons' for writing, and drama is a marvellous tool for providing contexts which not only motivate children to write but can also assist their understanding of the needs of the reader. Just as there are many approaches to teaching drama, as described in Chapter 3, so there are many ways in which writing activities can be linked to the drama.

The writer in role

When children write in role, they can benefit in various ways. Let us consider these by looking at the example of a child filling in a booking form for a holiday. They are in role as a travel agent. Benefits to working in this way include:

- **providing the writing task with a real sense of purpose** i.e. the form will be for a customer who is also in role
- **developing an understanding of when and why to use particular skills** e.g. fills in the form neatly because it is an important document

- **using reference skills as part of the role** e.g. checks the spelling of a town in the brochure
- **relating the format to the purpose** i.e. is learning when to use a particular format and also how to write in that format
- **making links between reading and writing** e.g. answering questions which are written on the form
- **using real texts as models** e.g. finding files, booking forms and information from brochures
- **providing an audience for the writing** e.g. the customer for checking or a 'clerk' at head office who then issues the tickets.

A further bonus is the high motivational factors involved when children work in this way because it is fun, non threatening, it is pretending to be a grown-up (which children of all ages usually love to do!) and it has a 'real' purpose. Such an atmosphere for learning is productive and effective, providing that the intended learning outcomes are carefully planned and monitored.

Another important feature of the 'writer in role' model is that it helps the child develop an empathy with the writer in ways which are particularly valuable for certain genres. The examples that follow show extracts of children's writing which have been written in role in response to an experience which has also happened in role. The first is a poem by Laura (age six years) which has been written after an exploration of how animals in zoos might feel about people staring at them all day. Laura wrote the poem in the role of a kangaroo. The second extract is from a memo written by Claire (age eleven years), in role as a factory worker, to the managing director to complain about the dangers of passive smoking in the staff rest-room. Each of these pieces was written after preparatory improvisational work (each taking ten minutes including discussion), designed specifically for the purpose of creating stimuli and empathy for the writing.

No matter how imaginative we believe children to be, they will always produce writing of a higher quality if we provide good stimuli for writing. If we expect children to write we need to give them something worthwhile to write about, and improvisations such as these are a valuable source of raw material with which the imagination can play.

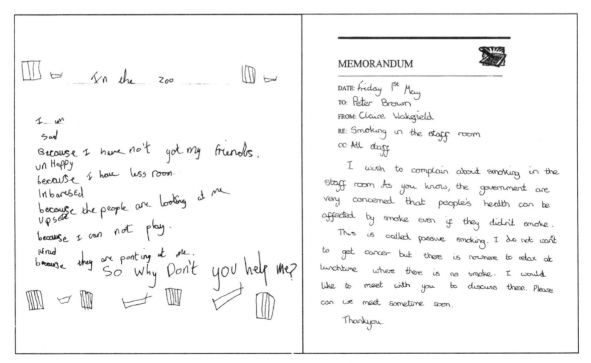

Figure 8.1 Written by Laura in the role of a kangaroo

Figure 8.2 A memo by Claire in role as a factory worker

Audience awareness

The other half of the writing equation is, of course, the reader, or audience, of the text. The drama can provide an audience for the writing in addition to (or even instead of) providing an audience for the drama itself. If children are going to learn how to meet the needs of different audiences by writing in a range of ways they need to understand the intended readers' perspectives. This is what is known as 'accommodating the audience' (Frank 1990), and can be done in three main ways.

1. Teacher in role If you are in role, requiring writing from the children for a purpose relating to that role, their thought processes will be extended into a more analytical mode of cognition. In other words, the writing process will actively involve the children in taking your needs as a reader into consideration. For example, you are in role as the hen (*Rosie's Walk*, Pat Hutchins 1970). You tell the children about what a wonderful walk you've just had, totally unaware of the dangers of the fox. They may try to warn you about the fox, but you don't believe them. Out of role, you then discuss how they might help Rosie, by writing to her. How could they write? Letters? Warning posters around the farm? Notes pinned to fences? Provide paper of different sizes and a range of writing materials for them to do their writing. Set a time limit. 'Rosie will be back in ten minutes! See how well you can write your warnings, and we'll give them to her when she returns…'. (Or you might pin them around the room for Rosie to read as she enacts her farmyard stroll. She will, of course, respond to the posters or letters! Reading these with the children is linking the writing and reading in a most productive way.) This example almost always results in the children then wanting to write to the fox!

2. Reading in role The children read texts in role first and discuss their responses. They then write for the reader whose role they have just taken. For example, in role as sorters at the Post Office, they have to decipher some badly written envelopes (which you provide). The envelopes are confusing because the handwriting is poor and the punctuation is used incorrectly. Ask them to decode the envelopes and make new labels in their best handwriting to stick over the top so the postman or postwoman will know where to deliver the letters.

3. Interactional roles This is where children are playing roles in which they have to write for each other or to each other. For example, in role as two characters from a story, letter writing could become an on-going activity. Providing a postbox, and pigeon holes for delivery adds to the excitement of this.

4. Reader research In this approach, the children do research in role, then write in another role or out of role. For example, in pairs they role-play market research interviews between magazine writers and teenagers about the sorts of things that teenagers like to know about pop stars. The writers make notes. After four minutes, they change roles and change partners, so that everyone ends up with a set of notes. Finally, in a third different partnership, the two look at the notes and write an article (out of role) about an imaginary pop star using the ideas given by the potential 'readers' of the magazine. Examples of such magazines should be available to examine for style, content and presentation.

Editing in role

Editing writing can sometimes seem a tedious task, especially for younger children. Indeed, it is not always necessary to write more than one draft – it depends on the nature of the writing. However, when writing does need to be put through several organisational processes (plan – first draft – edit – second draft – seek response – final draft – proof read – publish) it can help to create roles which will help the children to see the purpose of the process and also to make it more interesting. Examples of this might include:

- doctor's notes onto a report card (role-play area)
- exchanging work and 'marking' in role as the teacher
- birthday card designers planning in teams
- newspaper teams with editorial control
- practising handwriting in a Victorian classroom.

Positioning of the drama

There is no single formula for how the drama relates to the writing. One way of considering the variety of options open to you is to think about the position of the drama in relation to the writing. There are three identifiable places where the drama might fit.

1. Writing before the drama Writing in preparation for drama, for example the children are asked to write letters which bring some good news. The letters are then placed in a box and mixed up. The children are organised into groups of four representing a family having breakfast. One member of the family goes to collect a letter (randomly chosen from the box) and the children improvise their response.

2. Writing during the drama The writing takes place in role during the drama, either as a spontaneous response to the action, or as an event which you have planned into the activity. The most obvious place for this to happen is in the role-play area, as children write appointments, messages, lists, notes and so on as part of their play. However, the quality of this will depend very much on the provision. The home corner which has telephone directories, memo pads, headed notepaper, envelopes, address books, greetings cards etc. will promote far more developmental writing activities than the home corner which does not.

3. Writing after the drama The use of drama as a stimulus for writing has already been mentioned briefly. The strength of children's writing will nearly always relate to the quality of input beforehand. Children who have explored the theme of bullying through drama are likely to go on to write poetry with more depth of understanding and feeling than those who are told to write 'from cold'.

Using drama to teach writing in your literacy hour

During your daily hour of literacy, the 'wide range of strategies' which the NLS framework expects you to adopt in your teaching approach can and should include drama where appropriate. Drama helps to bring meaning to the language work you are teaching, and can provide multiple contexts for working with the range of texts required by the NLS framework. This does not mean that the drama takes over the whole hour. (Chapter 4 stresses the point that drama can take place within many different time-frames and group sizes.) Rather, it is used at an appropriate time during the hour to support and enhance the teaching, whilst maintaining the recommended time guidelines of the NLS Literacy Hour. Examples of appropriate activities are provided in Chapter 11.

Using drama as writing develops

Teaching strategies should be linked to the developmental stages of children's learning. A particularly useful model for the development of writing has been researched and developed by the Education Department of Western Australia (Raison 1994). This 'Developmental Continuum' is now offered to teachers as part of the wider language programme known as *First Steps*. This programme identifies clusters of 'key indicators' which describe certain writing behaviours typical of each stage. These are offered as an alternative to a linear sequence, as children tend to exhibit certain groups of behaviours within each stage, and these are not necessarily sequential. The phases of writing development established by this research are:

Phase 1   Role-play writing
Phase 2   Experimental writing
Phase 3   Early writing
Phase 4   Conventional writing
Phase 5   Proficient writing
Phase 6   Advanced writing

Another such framework has been developed during work with student teachers at Oxford Brookes University (Clipson-Boyles 1996). This is used in Figure 8.3 to demonstrate how drama might support children's writing at different stages of their development.

Fiction and non-fiction

The range of texts which children should encounter in connection with reading and writing (see Chapter 7 for a useful list – Categories of Texts) can be covered well in drama. Story writing can develop out of prior drama activities (role-play, improvisation, simulation, dynamic duos etc.), and indeed the drama can really help the ideas to flow, grow and develop! Likewise, non-fiction texts, particular 'real world texts' such as documents, forms, adverts have an extremely comfortable place within drama. If real texts are there during the experience, they are providing good models of writing for the children to emulate.

Responses to children's writing

Children crave response. It motivates them, it teaches them and it completes the cycle of communication. Responses can come from a variety of sources: peers, other classes, other teachers, family, relatives, local businesses, media, visitors, famous people and so on. Of course you are the central person whose response perhaps children depend upon more than anyone else's, and you are also responsible for coordinating the range of potential responses from others.

Planning writing activities so that response is inbuilt can be a tremendously enriching contribution to the whole purpose. Here are two examples:

 EXAMPLE 1   ***Messages to the imp***

A naughty imp is hiding somewhere in your classroom. Every night he comes out and makes a mess (which you all find each morning). So far he has tipped paintbrushes onto the carpet, ripped some newspapers all over the floor, and emptied out the multilink. (Avoid paint and glue for this experience!) The children are encouraged to write messages to him about this situation. Needless to say, he writes messages back!

 EXAMPLE 2   ***Publishing stories***

If the children are making books for the reading corner, this might be done with you in role as editor, and they in role as real authors, formalising the process, and resulting in an interchange of comments, faxes, phone messages and so on!

Resources

Resources in schools do not always have to depend on funding. There are many items which can be obtained free and which support children's literacy. For instance, texts such as:

- information leaflets
- bus timetables
- newspapers
- magazines

- comics
- food packaging
- posters
- junk mail

- flyers
- tickets
- receipts
- telephone directories.

These can be used in drama to model writing structures, and to use in children's play and role-play.

Computer-generated resources

Most software these days offers ready-made formats for writing. Even if you reproduce these to be filled in by hand for planning, they can offer plausible frameworks for children's writing which feel important and valid.

Writing areas

Setting up writing areas in classrooms is now common practice. A good selection of different types of paper and writing materials, to tempt the children to write, booths where they can hide away and so on. Developing this into an 'office' can further enhance the area and encourage children to write in role using ideas of their own. Equipment in this area might include:

- forms to fill in
- receipt books
- memo pads
- telephone message pads (see Appendix 4)
- dictionaries
- phone directories
- computer
- e-mail simulation (if you don't yet have the real thing)
- pretend fax machines
- typewriters
- message books
- post box
- a pigeonhole for each child.

Every school has parents who work in offices or own companies which may be willing to provide office stationery and texts to add to the authenticity. Often, companies discard large quantities of stationery when they change their logo or image for example.

So, in conclusion...

Writing activities should offer children opportunities to write under direction, in collaboration and independently. Drama offers all these options, and can result in truly motivated children who regard themselves confidently as writers, and can aim for high standards through modelling their writing on real texts.

PHASE	CHARACTERISTICS	REQUIREMENTS OF THE DRAMA
Stage 1: The Emergent Writer	● knows that print carries meaning ● writes for different purposes as part of play activities ● discriminates between writing and drawing ● writes some letters and similar shapes	To role-play reading activities, and start to focus on writing and saying words during the play.
Stage 2: The Exploratory Writer	○ understands link between sounds and symbols ○ invents spellings based on that understanding ○ leaves spaces between words ○ perceives self as a writer and reads own writing aloud ○ understands directionality	To write for others who will read their texts as part of the play. To use other resources containing texts as part of the play. To focus on concepts of sentence.
Stage 3: The Communicative Writer	● writes texts which can be read by others ● seeks information from range of sources (e.g. letters from books, posters, labels) ● understands sentence units ● will sometimes correct or edit work after reading through	To work with a range of formats for different purposes.
Stage 4: The Reflective Writer	○ adapts style according to purpose and audience ○ checks, reconsiders and redrafts own work ○ recognises the need for correct punctuation, spelling and grammar ○ evaluates the communicative effectiveness of own writing	To study real texts and model writing techniques in role, including editing, proof reading and producing texts for final publication.
Stage 5: The Versatile Writer	● adapts style according to purpose and audience ● moves text around to reorganise ideas ● uses ambitious vocabulary ● uses complex sentence structures	To provide contexts which will extend the boundaries of reasons to write into areas which will require more challenging styles, frameworks and vocabulary.

Figure 8.3 Drama activities for the developmental stages of writing

Chapter 9

Drama and Children Learning English as an Additional Language

Drama makes language learning enjoyable and lively and rescues second language learners from the fearful and soul-destroying clutches of boring pedagogues.   (Kallie 1991)

In this chapter you can read about:

- what teachers need to know about language diversity
- why the processes of drama are especially effective for second language learners
- the value of story to second language learners
- drama modes which are particularly useful for second language learners
- how drama can help all children to develop knowledge about language
- drama and multi-cultural education.

Language diversity in Britain

As the cultural diversity enjoyed by many European and North American urban areas continues to develop in Britain, we become increasingly aware of the wide range of languages spoken by children in our schools. This rich tapestry of linguistic patterning can be an asset to any language curriculum. It enables children to observe and explore language within the context of actual usage and relate this directly to the cultures and traditions of different groups, including the cross-cultural integration within their own communities.

However, there are important educational implications for those children who are learning English as a second language, and the first of these is to recognise that diversity requires high levels of teacher understanding. The problem with such labels as 'bilingual learners', 'English as a second language' (ESL), and 'mother tongue' is that they can imply vast generalities about these children which are not always accurate. This can sometimes result in basic stereotyping and, as a consequence, inappropriate teaching approaches.

The reality is that the whole area of bilingualism is complex. For instance, the term might include third generation children in stable well-established families, children in transient families whose parents are planning to settle in Britain for temporary periods of work, or newly-arrived families escaping from political unrest in their homeland. The status of English also varies enormously within groups. Some families may use two languages, including English at home, some children may be the only speakers of English in their family, commencing from when they start school; some may have parents who speak two languages including English but are new to English themselves; others may belong to families where everyone speaks their community language in the home and English outside the home. These are only a few examples of the numerous variations, so the teacher's task is not merely to establish the actual languages spoken by the children in their class, but also the part which they play in the lives of the children and the customs and practices which accompany them.

Communication styles vary not only in the words spoken but also in the ways in which they are spoken. The rise and fall of tone, speed, volume, the way in which discourse is constructed, listening postures and other body language are all potent forces behind cultural differences. A knowledge of these helps the teacher to understand and respect the whole language of the child, whilst at the same time to teach the styles of English, not as better or superior ways, but as different ways. Viv Edwards (1995) also stresses the importance of understanding naming practices, and ensuring that children's names are pronounced correctly. For example, should the form of address be the last name or the first? Is the name on school records the religious name or the family name? Should any of the names be used by family only, and so on. Such considerations can all be addressed through adequate teacher knowledge and the recognition that respectful consideration of such issues makes a significant difference to the child's sense of security and willingness to learn.

However, even when all these tangible elements of diversity are addressed, there is an even more complex set of dynamics at work which must be considered by the teacher. Language does not exist in a self-contained vacuum. It inter-relates with all human activity, and at the heart of that activity is learning.

Language and learning

Language is inextricably linked to learning because we use language to think. The development of conceptual understanding and the growth of knowledge in all areas of the curriculum depend on the frameworks of language needed to explain, describe, discuss and challenge them. We use language to construct meaning, to dismantle meaning, and to redesign meaning. We use it to recall, remember, hypothesise, predict and so on. Clearly, where English is the only instructional language for the curriculum, EAL pupils are not only learning a new language but are also trying to contextualise all their other learning within that language rather than in their own.

Studies in the United States have shown that where EAL pupils and their majority language peers were taught together in two languages across the curriculum, the EAL pupils made much better progress than those taught in an all-English programme (Collier 1996). The main reason for this was the fact that the EAL pupils were able to use their first language in order to develop concepts and skills, and as they continued to do this alongside English, the two eventually became interchangeable.

It would be impractical to expect such bilingual teaching to take place in all schools, particularly in classes where there is more than one language spoken in addition to English. However, Collier acknowledges that important elements of her research can be transported into everyday classroom practice. These include 'a multi-cultural perspective, collaborative, interactional learning, and a high level of cognitive challenge' (ibid.). The educational implications here are very different from policies imposed some years ago when it was thought best to exclude the home language from the educational process. It is now recognised by many that in fact the home language has a vital role to play in the child's learning, and that giving the language status, taking an active interest in it and allowing the child to use it alongside English will help the child's progress, not only in language but also in their conceptual development across all subjects.

Drama and language learning

Drama requires active involvement, and can accommodate the integration of reading, writing and oracy in relevant and realistic contexts. It helps children to make sense of language and meaning, and offers the option of repetition in fun ways which can take the labour out of tasks which require high levels of revision and recap. It provides situations in which children are required to construct knowledge, while at the same time offering the flexibility to revise and reconstruct that same knowledge. All this takes place through listening, experimenting, reworking, modelling and imitating.

Drama enables children to work together in groups and involves high levels of discussion which leads directly to the development of ideas and concepts relating to both formal and informal linguistic situations. It also enables EAL pupils to use their first language alongside English. Drama can be used to assist learning in various areas of the curriculum and thus offers a whole range of learning opportunities which can be used effectively in multilingual classrooms.

Identifying the learning needs of EAL pupils

Having taken the time and care to find out all there is to know about the language background of the child, as described in the first section of this chapter, it is necessary to ascertain the level of fluency in English. Education authorities have different ways of categorising EAL pupils, but one of the most commonly used systems is that developed by Hilary Hester at the Centre for Language in Primary Education and recommended by the Home Office for Section 11 reporting purposes. This uses a framework called the Stages of English Learning and is intended to provide a continuum which builds on the developing achievements of the child. The Stages are detailed under four headings:

Stage 1: new to English
Stage 2: becoming familiar with English
Stage 3: becoming confident as a user of English
Stage 4: a very fluent user of English in most social and learning contexts.

Identifying the current level of fluency enables the teacher to plan the types of learning experiences which will most help the child. The key principle here is integration, which needs to happen at three levels.

- **Firstly, total integration of EAL pupils into the classroom** (rather than learning in separate outside groups) is now the norm. This is in recognition of the fact that when we learn language we need exposure to it in addition to practice in its use. It also plays an important part by including the home languages of these pupils in ongoing classroom life, to assist their conceptual progress, to enrich the linguistic understanding of other children in the class, and to promote a truly multi-cultural ethos.
- **Secondly, an integrated approach to language** is at the heart of good practice in primary English teaching for all children, as specified in the National Curriculum Order for English (1995). Where the connections between oracy, reading and writing are continually being made, explicitly and implicitly, roots of understanding grow deeper and feed the ongoing growth of language and literacy.
- **Finally, the integration between language teaching and subject teaching** is vital if learning opportunities are to be maximised. For instance, role-play about a history topic helps children to use the language of the subject whilst at the same time developing their understanding of the content. This might also then be extended into a writing or reading activity which draws on the material from that role-play experience.

However, all these considerations should be underpinned with a sound knowledge of language acquisition. In relation to drama, the key principles of language learning include:

- meaningful contexts for the language (e.g. role-play in a shop)
- listening to the patterns of language (e.g. watching others perform their work)
- active participation (e.g. group planning)
- use of supportive resources (e.g. puppets)
- imitation of appropriate modelling (e.g. group improvisation)
- repetition (e.g. re-reading play scripts)
- use of the home language (e.g. bilingual theatre/translation)
- motivation and security (e.g. the fun of drama).

The power of the group

Language cannot be learned in isolation. It is a dynamic process which requires interaction between people. It therefore makes good educational sense to allow children to work collaboratively in groups where they can speak in a range of ways and learn to listen to one another. However, successful group management is a real challenge for the teacher if the children are to stay on task and engage with each other in ways which will help them to learn.

Groupings for drama will vary in size as already described in Chapter 4. When considering the needs of EAL pupils there will also be the issue of levels of fluency and understanding to consider. Groupings will change according to the purpose of the activity and the particular learning needs of the individual. Here are some examples:

1. **Grouped with speakers of the same language:** to discuss and role-play ideas in the home language. Perform to others in home language with an English narration provided by a Stage 2 or 3 pupil.
2. **Grouped with monolingual English speakers:** to discuss and role-play ideas in English, with the possibility to translate into home language for others to hear.
3. **Mixed fluency plus English speaking group:** to enable more fluent bilingual children to translate and interpret.

Drama and story

Arguably, story is at the heart of all language learning. Stories have been told since history began, passed down through the ages, between generations and across cultures, many written down to be read. Every day, people can be heard telling real-life stories of things which have happened to them or others, and stories, real and imagined, are encapsulated in songs, poems and on television and cinema screens.

Stories transmit ideas, customs and traditions, but they also transmit language – meaning, vocabulary, sounds of rhythm and rhyme, sentence and narrative structure are all communicated through stories. So it is small wonder that telling and reading stories to children in school has long been considered to be an important part of primary education. Stories can also be used in other ways to teach language skills and drama has a useful part to play in offering a more active understanding in the following ways:

- miming the actions as the story is read
- miming the story as child retells in home language
- performing the story in English with child translator
- performing the story in home language with child translator
- puppet replay of the story
- improvising alternative endings to the story
- introducing new character into the story
- watching a professional performance of a story
- watching a film or TV performance of a story
- using cue cards with phrases from the story to make a new story.

These approaches should also be used with stories from a variety of cultures, and encouraging children to bring in stories from home doesn't merely expand your story supply but also gives encouraging messages to children about the status and value of their home language.

Working in role

There are different ways of working in role, as described in Chapter 3, and you should refer to these for more detailed descriptions of how you might use them. When teaching EAL pupils, working in role has four particular benefits which meet their language learning needs appropriately and effectively. These are:

1. the provision of 'real' contexts for the language
2. opportunities to hear others modelling the appropriate language
3. opportunities to practise language and take risks with new vocabulary and constructions in an enjoyable and non-threatening situation
4. opportunities to 're-run' or 'repeat' language scenarios in order to practise fluency, expression, and build confidence.

Reading plays

This activity clearly depends on the children's level of reading ability, but can be a good supporting bridge between dependent and independent reading. Plays can be read in different ways: in unison, in pairs, independently as characters etc. Reading a play through several times gives the opportunity to practise fluency and expression, and adding movements and gestures not only makes it more fun but also entails discussion and explanation within the group, which is itself part of the learning process.

Puppets

There are different ways of making and using puppets, and these are explained in Chapter 3. Puppets are an extremely useful resource to assist language learning for EAL pupils. Commercially produced puppets can be used to accompany the reading of books, listening to tapes and for spontaneous improvisation. An interesting and adaptable collection kept in the classroom is usually a tremendous stimulus for children, and a commercial or home-made puppet theatre can offer a 'safe' environment within which to explore and practise language. Some publishers sell puppets to accompany their reading schemes, and these can also provide additional access to meaning in the texts which children are reading.

Structuring the children's work around known stories, including those from different cultures, can also provide a scaffold on which to build their own stories. Puppets which the children make themselves offer a further host of valuable learning experiences. Firstly, the actual planning, designing and making of the puppets provides a context for using the language, not only of the technology curriculum, but also of the story for which the puppets are intended. In other words, the story vocabulary assists the technology and the technology vocabulary assists the exploration of the story. For instance, descriptions of a character's appearance and behaviour, scene setting for any background models, ways in which they will need to move in order to express their personality and so on will all be discussed in the course of this work.

Moving on to the work entailed in planning the actual performance, the children will be involved in re-telling the story, sequencing the events and creating their own spoken lines, with or without a narrator. Characterisation of the voices also provides scope for practising fluency, speed, volume, expression and intonation, and an awareness of the needs of an audience will have to be addressed.

Masks

Many of the learning processes described in the previous section on puppets are also true of masks. The difference lies in the fact that a mask enables the child to use movement and gesture as well as voice. This is useful when children are role-playing within a particular situation but lack confidence. A mask can literally be a place to hide whilst exploring new language, thus adding an element of fun but also a feeling of 'safety'. Masks can be used in free role-play and improvisation, but are also useful when children are presenting their work to others.

Mime

Mime can provide an active visual resource to accompany stories or explanations. It can also provide a framework for transferring thoughts, ideas or instructions into gesture. These approaches offer ways of supporting the language and learning of EAL pupils, both from the use of mime by the teacher and also the use of mime by the children themselves. There are various contexts within which mime might be used. Here are some examples:

- after a story
- during a story
- during the setting of a task
- during an explanation
- as part of a question and answer session
- as an end-product to a piece of work
- when giving feedback.

The mime in each of these contexts could be organised in different ways. For instance:

- teacher instructs – child or children mime
- teacher mimes – child guesses
- pupils instruct each other to mime
- pupils plan and prepare a mime for others
- pupils read and mime cue cards for others to guess.

The mime might be used for short caption-type activities such as explaining vocabulary (e.g. prepositions, direction, speed), changing the meaning of same-phrase construction (e.g. 'She is cleaning her teeth. Now she is washing her face. Now she is drying her face.') and revisiting vocabulary (e.g. recapping on common occupations). The mime may take the form of short captions (words or phrases) for explanation, demonstration or guessing. Alternatively it may be presented in longer sequences to show to the rest of the group or class.

Modelling from videos and cassettes

There have been many commercial products aimed at teaching foreign languages through recorded training programmes, listening, repeating and checking all being important processes in the learning. Doing this individually has its limits, although the interactive software now available for multi-media computers has tried to address some of these by offering the additional dimension of recording the learner's voice and giving feedback. However, using with the technology with a partner can be much more rewarding.

Listening to a short tape together, or watching a very short clip of video which can be replayed, can provide contexts for role-play. For example, the teacher could record a conversation between a waiter/waitress and customer in a cafe which might go something like this:

Waiter:	Good morning. Can I help you?
Customer:	Good morning. Please may I see the menu.
Waiter:	Yes, of course. Here you are.
Customer:	Mmmmm. Please may I have a cup of coffee and a cheese sandwich.
Waiter:	Brown bread or white bread?
Customer:	White please.
Waiter:	OK. Thank you.

Two children could replay the tape as often as they like, and play with the dialogue themselves in the role-play area which would be set up as a cafe. Recording their own dialogue, and listening to check, could be an additional part of the activity. Playing their 'best' final version to the teacher would provide evidence of their work, and going on to order different things in the cafe would be an appropriate extension of their work.

Drama and multi-cultural education

Regardless of the cultural mix of a school, it is important for all children to learn about the diverse and interesting mixture of our multi-cultural society here in Britain. Helping children to develop knowledge and understanding about the rich variety of customs, foods, languages, stories and religions can make an important contribution towards building a harmonious and peaceful society in which differences are respected and the diversity celebrated.

Drama can be of great support to such work. At the surface informational level, it can be used to impart knowledge through interaction. For example, the simulation approach to teaching about a Christian wedding provided in Chapter 3 could be used to enable children to experience a different cultural festival. However, at a deeper level, drama is also an invaluable way to approach more difficult issues, particularly with older children. The activity example using Jackie Kay's poem 'Duncan Gets Expelled' (1994) which is about racist bullying, also described in Chapter 3, offers a powerful way to introduce this topic.

The vital points to remember when planning for multi-cultural education are:

- MCE should be provided for all
- MCE should work towards understanding through information
- MCE should offer a celebration of diversity rather than aiming towards homogenisation!
- MCE should not be afraid to tackle difficult issues
- MCE should always aim for positive outcomes.

Drama has a role to play in all these things, by acquiring knowledge through experience, empathy through active engagement, and offering a safety net of distance when dealing with sensitive issues.

Chapter 10

Assessment and Progression

Good assessment practice enables children to be able to fulfil their learning potential and raises self-esteem and self-confidence. (Sainsbury 1996)

In this chapter you can read about:

- the key characteristics of good assessment practice
- a framework for the assessment of drama
- assessment and the measurement of progression in drama
- using drama to make assessments in other areas of the curriculum.

Drama and assessment

Drama provides extremely appropriate opportunities for assessing speaking and listening within the curriculum for English, as shown in Chapter 6, and many of the reading and writing activities described in Chapters 7 and 8 can provide useful contexts and evidence for assessing literacy skills. However, drama is not only a vehicle for the assessment of oracy and literacy, although it has a valuable part to play in this. It is also an important discrete area in its own right, as identified within the English curriculum, and there are valuable areas of learning and development to be offered by drama as an arts subject.

If children are to gain the maximum benefit from drama you need to plan with a sound understanding of what you expect them to achieve. Effective planning works hand-in-hand with teacher expectations and assessment, so let us begin by looking at the key characteristics of good assessment practice.

Key characteristics of good assessment practice

Assessment takes time and skilful management, therefore it needs to be worth the effort! The best assessments are those which are useful. In particular, good assessment information should inform teacher and pupil about:

1. what the pupil can achieve competently
2. the progress which has been made.

The teacher should also be able to glean important information about:

3. the effectiveness of the teaching approach
4. where the learning needs to go next.

All these things can happen when the assessment is taking place as an integral part of teaching and learning, rather than just an additional component at the end of the activity, because there can be more interaction between teacher and pupils.

Integrating teaching, learning and assessment

Interaction means that instruction and feedback can be given as an ongoing part of the teaching, and children can respond accordingly. An integrated approach to assessment also means that the process can be assessed in addition to the product, and this is crucial if the teacher is to understand the full learning picture. Just as a piece of beautiful handwriting could belie a laborious process during which the pencil was held inappropriately and the letters formed from right to left, so a piece of thought-provoking and well-constructed drama might be the result of one dominant leader in a dysfunctional group rather than a collaborative effort. In both these examples, the teacher could make a glowing summative assessment of the end-product without being aware of the inadequate quality of the processes which were involved in their production.

Integrating assessment into everyday classroom activities encourages a reflective approach to teaching and learning and provides multi-faceted information which feeds into the educational process. This information might be from pupil to teacher (e.g. answering a question), from teacher to pupil (e.g. recapping on a point which has been misunderstood), from pupil to pupil (e.g. giving feedback), and self evaluation (e.g. pupil reflecting on her own outcomes).

Clarity about what is assessed

Another feature of good assessment is a clear understanding, by teacher and pupils, of what is being assessed. Teacher expectations should be made clear to children so that they know what they are aiming for, and can recognise their achievements. During a drama activity, which on the surface may appear to be an 'informal' learning situation, it is arguably even more important to make explicit to children what is required of them. So comments like:

- 'I shall be watching you all to see how carefully you are listening to each other.'
- 'It is important to get the sequence of events in the right order. I shall be asking the other children to comment on that when you show your story later.'
- 'The audience will need to hear you from the back of the hall, so I am going to stand there now to check if you are using your voices clearly and loudly, but without shouting.'
- 'When you've finished playing in the home corner, I want you to tell me about what your characters have been reading and writing.'

...all help the children to focus on the relevant learning points.

Useful evidence

Such clarity of purpose is also important when collecting evidence of children's progress. When conducting more summative forms of assessment, you need to be clear about how you will search the material to identify learning outcomes. So, with a scripted play written from an improvisation exercise, for example, you might be asking yourself any of the following questions:

- Have they used language which is appropriate to the situation?
- Have they provided implicit information in the dialogue?
- Have they included additional information to develop characters?
- Have they constructed a plausible ending during the sequence, as opposed to 'quickly finishing off' for convenience?

Asking yourself questions which can be clearly answered 'yes' or 'no', or with direct examples, is a helpful way to structure an assessment framework, and provides a more rigorous evaluation process than generalised statements such as, 'They presented a good improvisation.'

Another point to remember about the nature of summative evidence is that it can only tell you something useful if it can be compared with other evidence from a different phase. In other words, it needs to be part of a fuller picture which provides evidence of progression.

Progression and change

Progression in learning means that something changes. New knowledge is there, where it didn't exist before, a skill has appeared or improved, a concept has been acquired, can be explained, and so on. Skills are easier to measure than knowledge and concepts because they are observable whereas knowledge and concepts can only be observed within the contexts where they are being applied.

Seeing progression as evidence of change highlights the need to avoid deficit models of assessment which just identify 'gaps'. Gaps in a child's knowledge or competencies are only useful if they are considered within the context of a developmental continuum. In other words, if a gap coincides with the next stage of learning, then it is appropriate for it to be addressed. However, if it is too far along the sequential line of conceptual development it is usually more effective to provide other essential prerequisites for learning which are needed before the gap can be addressed.

Creating records which are useful

Good assessment requires record keeping which is systematic, easy to interpret, relevant and useful. Records can take many forms, some being the pupils' own documentary evidence and others being your own. The drama process might involve any of the following types of records:

- diary of theatre visits (ongoing from Year 1 to 6)
- tapes of dialogue
- video evidence
- self-evaluation forms
- written work relating to drama context (e.g. news report)
- skills continua tick lists.

(Photocopiable sheets are available in Appendix 4 for your use. These include theatre visit logs, reviews, and skills continua record sheets.)

Giving status to the learning

When children are worried about being tested, it is usually because they believe it to be so important that they will in some way be in trouble if they 'fail'. At the other end of the spectrum, drama can understandably be associated with leisure and pleasure, with the result that a laissez-faire attitude might be adopted towards it in schools. If drama is to be valued and respected by children, it is important that they recognise the place of assessment and the expectations which their teacher has within that framework. They also need to recognise that what they are doing is relevant to them personally. This can usually be achieved by making it explicit to the children that they are learning many useful skills in drama, by demonstrating that you are taking note of their learning, and perhaps most importantly, by giving them regular feedback on their progress.

Frameworks for assessing drama

In the absence of drama as a foundation subject within the National Curriculum, the Arts Council of Great Britain produced guidelines in a booklet called *Drama in Schools* (1992). This useful publication provides an important supplement to the requirements for drama outlined in the Order for English, by addressing drama 'as an art form with its own distinct discipline and methodology'. In addition to recommended programmes of study, it also includes guidance on continuity, progression and assessment including End of Key Stage Statements (see Appendix 3). These enable primary teachers to make summative assessments at the end of Years 2 and 6. The statements are divided into three categories, *Making, Performing* and *Responding,* and can offer a good general framework to schools who are developing a whole-school approach to planning and assessment of drama as a discrete art form.

However, the embedded nature of drama within English, alongside the other rich teaching and learning opportunities which it can offer, means that it is also possible to use a more detailed framework to maximise the potential of assessing learning during drama activities. The framework in this chapter is designed to save time by enabling you to maximise the assessment opportunities within drama and assess a wide range of skills and knowledge. The model also means that you can make continuous formative assessments throughout the primary years as well as summative assessments at the end of the key stages.

The framework is designed to fit appropriately into the primary curriculum where the integration and overlap of subject areas and learning activities are not only an inevitable part of sensible planning, but also help children to make logical connections and links between areas of knowledge.

The framework is divided into five Areas of Learning, each of which is divided into three Elements as shown in Figure 10.1. The five Areas provide excellent opportunities to assess drama from different perspectives because there is a rich interlinking of contexts. This doesn't mean introducing additional, more complex approaches to assessment for teachers who already feel over-burdened with paperwork. Rather, it means offering a model which addresses the discrete nature of drama as an art form, but which also enables you to assess English and other curriculum areas. In other words, this is a framework which facilitates useful integrated assessment rather than eliminating or restricting by 'specialist' labelling.

1 Operational skills	a) planning b) problem-solving c) working collaboratively
2 Communication skills	a) spoken language b) written language c) performance skills
3 Creative skills	a) use of imagination b) use of resources c) interpretation
4 Knowledge and understanding	a) character b) audience c) content
5 Responding	a) listening b) interpreting c) evaluating

Figure 10.1 Drama assessment framework

Before we look at the details of how children might be expected to progress through each of the Elements, let us first consider the significance of each of the five assessment Areas.

Area 1: Operational skills

Area 1 relates to the ways in which children work, independently and collaboratively. If we are concerned about whether children stay on task, can work towards targets, work with the ideas of others, can organise their work, plan tasks and material, set about solving problems and so on, then we need to assess them regularly to ensure that they are progressing in the right direction. Clearly, these skills can be assessed in many, if not all, subject areas, but drama is a particularly good place to do this systematically because operational skills have such a central part to play. Including them within an assessment framework makes these important aspects of personal development and learning more explicit, and it is likely you will find that, by focusing on them in drama, you will become much more aware of them at other times. Indeed, by making transparent to the children your assessments of Operational Skills during drama activities, you can also be encouraging them to transfer their 'expertise' to other regions of the curriculum!

Area 2: Communication skills

The overlap with English is particularly obvious in Area 2. The assessment of literacy and oracy is a vital part of the core curriculum, and drama is only one context within which this will take place. The assessment of performance skills also includes some integration of English skills. However, this Element offers opportunities to move into more specialist areas of drama and theatre arts. For example, assessing a child's voice projection and expression during an assembly for parents will address the speaking and listening requirements, but could also be considered to be part of performance.

Area 3: Creative skills

When we try to define the word 'imagination' it is tempting to think about creating something from nothing. But that can never be true. Our imagination draws upon our experience. It takes events from our memory, things we have seen, heard, read, discussed, smelt, felt and touched, both directly and indirectly (through the representations of others), and recreates them into new forms. Use of imagination, therefore, is about transferring knowledge and experience from one form into another. Likewise, the use of resources, musical instruments, audio equipment, lights, props, costumes etc. is not just about correct technical use. It is also about the consideration of what can be created *by* their use – mood, atmosphere, visual image and so on. By assessing children's creative skills, you will be helping them to grow and develop into interpretative thinkers who know that they have the power to influence the way they present and communicate their work and ideas.

Area 4: Knowledge and understanding

The first two Elements in Area 4 (*character and audience*) are very specific to drama. Understanding characters, whether it be from the perspective of a writer in role or the consideration of how a person might move, is an essential part of drama as experience and theatre as performance. Understanding the needs of an audience can also cover a range of levels; for example, writing in role involves selecting an appropriate genre for the intended reader, and portraying the movement of a character is helping the audience to understand and believe in that character.

The third Element of Area 4, *content*, is a generic category which can be applied to different subject areas. So, for instance, during a simulation of a voyage with Francis Drake, you might be assessing the children's knowledge of Tudor life and concepts of exploration. On the other hand, during the development of improvised scenes from *Macbeth* you could be assessing their knowledge of Shakespearian theatre.

Area 5: Responding

In Area 5, *listening*, *analysing* and *evaluating* all have an explicit place in English but also have appropriate applications in other areas. Recognising how sounds can be used in different ways for effect in a particular scene links directly to the National Curriculum Order for music, using photographs from the past to create tableaux involves interpretation in history, and evaluating the accuracy of a reporter's 'television piece' about the effects of a volcanic eruption relates appropriately to the National Curriculum Order for geography. In addition to subject specific examples, it is also clear that the skills in this Area are vital to the general principals of the learning process, for example evaluation is an important part of all subjects.

Arguably, 'response' is at the heart of all learning. It is about how children *show* what they have learned, how children *apply* their learning and how children *assimilate* and *adapt* their learning to other contexts. It is therefore an extremely useful Area to assess in order to monitor children's personal application to the learning process.

Progression: a whole-school approach

As with the assessment of all areas of learning, it is important to relate your assessments directly to progression. If assessment exists within a vacuum, unrelated to what has been achieved in the past and disconnected from what is planned for the next learning stages, then its value is questionable. No matter how excellent a teacher might be within the confines of her own classroom, there is much research to show that a whole-school approach, where staff work as a team and where progression is monitored along commonly-agreed continua, creates the optimum impact on pupils' learning (Rossi and Stringfield 1995; Kane and Khattri 1995). A whole school approach to drama requires helpful guidance on how children might be expected to make progress during their six years in school. This, combined with vertical planning of drama teaching methods can result in a balanced approach which develops fully the potential of drama in the creative arts, in English and in other subject areas.

Figure 10.2 offers six developmental competencies for each Element in the framework. These are not necessarily intended to run parallel to the six years of primary schooling, as children will inevitably progress at different rates. They are, however, intended to provide a **starting point** for measurement within the different assessment areas.

As with any tool offered to teachers, it is important for you to use this progression chart flexibly in ways which are appropriate to your school context. For example, if your school is only in the early stages of developing a drama policy, it may be wise to select just some of the competencies to start with, then add to these gradually. Likewise, you may wish to substitute some of the prescribed competencies with others of your choice which you feel to be more appropriate to the children in your school. The important thing to remember is that an assessment framework should not drive you in directions which are unproductive or even impossible – it should assist you in providing what is best for the children, and this will almost always involve an amount of adaptation and development.

Assessing other curriculum areas through drama

The Drama Assessment Framework enables you to plan and assess drama in ways which:

- address the requirements for drama in the Order for English
- make use of drama opportunities to teach other English skills
- develop drama as an artistic discipline
- maximise the advantages of employing drama to teach other subjects.

Throughout this book, there is reference to the generic nature of drama which enables other areas of the curriculum, and in particular English, to be taught. Such application of drama in the primary school is also true of assessment. During drama activities, observations of children's skills and understandings can be used to make evaluations about their current levels of learning in other subjects.

OPERATIONAL SKILLS

A) Planning
- can make independent decisions about tasks in a role-play area
- can brainstorm ideas then sort into logical groupings
- can plan at least three tasks in sequence to achieve an objective
- can plan a presentation using own ideas
- can plan a short performance including use of additional resources

B) Problem-solving
- can break down a problem into component parts
- can speculate about the effects of a solution
- can describe the problem from different perspectives
- can offer a range of solutions which address different perspectives
- can use reference materials to find information to solve a problem
- can discriminate between different approaches to different types of problem

C) Working Collaboratively
- can discuss and plan with a partner
- can offer ideas to a group of three or more
- can change ideas after listening to others
- can suggest appropriate roles to different group members
- can express disagreement constructively
- can address and help to resolve group conflict constructively

COMMUNICATION SKILLS

A) Spoken Language
- can express an idea or opinion in role
- can change the mode of speaking for a change of character
- can adopt a more formal tone in an appropriate role
- can communicate the ideas of a character clearly to an audience
- can use Standard English appropriately in role
- can express opinions using supporting evidence in Standard English and other forms

B) Written Language
- can use writing conventions in role for specific purposes
- can write brainstorming charts and sort into lists
- can write in role from multiple perspectives
- can write in range of genres for multiple imagined audiences
- can write instructions narratives and scripts for presentations and performance
- can write in direct speech, indirect speech and script form

C) Performance Skills
- can perform action replays of characters in role-play area for teacher
- can present mime and puppet representations to the class
- can represent different characterisations to rest of class
- can project voice to larger audience (e.g. in assembly)
- can present appropriate voice and movement of characters to a larger audience
- can explore different approaches to voice, gesture and emotion of character

CREATIVE SKILLS

A) Use of Imagination
- can introduce ideas from stories into role-play
- can organise ideas into a short mime or puppet play
- can invent alternative endings to stories and plays
- can organise own ideas into a short play on a given theme
- can bring different ideas to a given theme
- can develop ways of communicating ideas on a theme of their choice

B) Use of Resources
- can select costumes and props appropriate to role during play
- can discuss character features when designing puppets and masks
- can use appropriate resources for sound effects
- can decide on appropriate props, costumes and sound effects to enhance performance
- can select and use different recorded music to create atmosphere

C) Interpretation
- can recreate a story in role-play area
- can transfer learning between drama and other subjects
- can interpret dialogue and stage directions from a play script
- can discuss themes in plays performed by professionals
- can transfer style elements from professional theatre into their own drama
- can make links between approaches to presentation and themes

UNDERSTANDING

A) Character
- can talk about a character played in a role
- can discuss the difference between real and imagined characters
- understands that people can have different perspectives on the same event
- can express an opinion which is different to their own
- can explore movement and voice of characters
- can explore character motivation within situations

B) Audience
- can extend role-play to show the teacher
- presents confidently to the class
- presents confidently to a larger audience
- can communicate the ideas of a character clearly to an audience
- considers the aural needs of the audience
- considers the visual perspectives of the audience
- understands that individuals in an audience will respond differently

C) Content
- can discuss the sequence of events after role-play
- can use prior learning in the drama
- can research information for the drama
- can identify further research neds after the drama
- can present key facts in dramatic form
- can interpret key facts from different perspectives

RESPONDING

A) Listening
- listens to a partner in role and responds appropriately
- watches the work of others and remembers key points
- can discuss different ideas or issues which have been presented in a drama
- ask appropriate questions arising from what has been heard
- can distinguish between different types of speech including Standard English
- Recalls things heard on a previous occasion to use in discussion

B) Analysing
- justifies reasons for choices and decisions in role-play
- discusses feelings and thoughts about particular characters
- can discuss how they felt as a particular character
- can predict how a different character might have felt
- can compare how two different characters might have felt about the same event
- discusses reasons for the style of presentation by professionals

C) Evaluating
- discuss at least two things they like about a piece, and why
- can support discussions of things they don't like with ideas for improvement
- compare two pieces on the same theme
- evaluate their own work against the teacher's expectations
- can compare their work with previous pieces
- can identify alternative approaches which might have been better

Figure 10.2 Progression of competencies for drama

For easy reference, Figure 10.3 lists each of the 15 Elements and suggests where they can be used to assess:

(a) Drama/Theatre Studies
(b) English
(c) Other subject areas

Element	Drama	English	Other subjects
OPERATIONAL SKILLS			
Planning	✓	✓	✓
Problem solving	✓	✓	✓
Working Collaboratively	✓	✓	✓
COMMUNICATION SKILLS			
Spoken Language	✓	✓	✗
Written Language	✓	✓	✗
Performance Skills	✓	✗	✗
CREATIVE SKILLS			
Use of Imagination	✓	✓	✗
Use of Resources	✓	✗	✗
Interpretation	✓	✓	✗
UNDERSTANDING			
Character	✓	✓	✗
Audience	✓	✓	✗
Content	✓	✓	✓
RESPONDING			
Listening	✓	✓	✗
Analysing	✓	✓	✗
Evaluating	✓	✓	✗

Figure 10.3 Assessment potentials of the Elements

- A tick indicates that the Element offers assessment criteria relating to the subject area.
- A cross indicates that the potential for assessment will not link directly to curriculum content (although there might be general application possibilities).

In the first column (drama), all the Elements are ticked because this is an assessment framework for drama!

In the second column (English), all Elements are ticked except *Performance Skills* and *Use of Resources* (because the competencies described in Figure 10.2 for these two are particularly geared towards theatre studies). This demonstrates the huge potential for teaching and assessing English through drama activities.

In the third column (other subjects), all three *Operational Skills* Elements are ticked as these are generic skills which fit appropriately into other parts of the curriculum. The other ticked Element is *Content*. This is the most obvious area to be assessing children in other areas of the curriculum during drama. For example, a simulation of a Victorian classroom provides opportunities to check children's understanding of appropriate language and behaviour for that period, and accounts of

Victorian home-life as the children respond in role to your questions. Likewise, the improvised questioning of a partner in role after an imaginary visit to a particular place (which has been researched by both pupils beforehand) could test the use of geographical terminology and/or knowledge of that place.

It is quite possible for you to adapt this approach to the Framework if you wish. For instance *Listening*, *Analysing* and *Evaluating* clearly have a part to play in other areas of the curriculum, but have not been ticked here for assessment because the competencies listed in Figure 10.2 relate directly to responses to theatre and drama. You could, however, develop your own competency lists which relate to subject areas instead. The Framework is intended to be flexible. Figure 10.3 is provided here, not to define tightly how you should be working, but rather to help you gain an insight into the potential for assessment during drama activities and to provide suggestions and starting points for the development of your own assessment designs.

Chapter 11

Planning a Whole-School Approach to Drama

To ensure continuity in drama, pupils require clear learning goals and frequent opportunities to reflect upon their work. They should always be able to place what they are learning in the wider context of the drama curriculum as a whole.　　　　(The Arts Council of Great Britain 1992)

In this chapter you can read about:

- the importance of developing a cohesive team plan for drama
- a whole-school approach to theatre visits and record keeping
- the role of the drama coordinator
- suggested activities for each term which link to NLS text ranges.

Whole-school drama

Introducing drama as a whole-school approach is challenging, particularly when staff feel unsure about their abilities to teach drama. Planning this as a team has many benefits. You can ensure that coverage is developmental and varied to suit the needs of the children at each stage. This also adds strength to what you are building because the children will be accumulating skills and knowledge as they move through the school which will underpin the new approaches introduced. Team planning provides mutual support, where ideas can be shared and discussed and suggestions offered. But perhaps most importantly, a staff who work together in a holistic way with agreed aims, commitment and enthusiasm can have an astounding impact on the quality of the learning, as demonstrated in the Success For All programme in USA (Slavin *et al.* 1996). For, whilst talented individual teachers might offer a memorable year of drama to their own class, the value of that learning will be the proverbial drop in the ocean! In comparison, six years of progressive drama education during which they are developing competencies in a targeted range of skills are going to produce pupils who are confident and creative learners with a good knowledge of theatre arts and a sense of ownership and control of language and drama as an expressive form. Such planning ideally needs to take place under the guidance of a designated drama coordinator.

The role of the drama coordinator

Headteachers who offer this role to a staff member are acknowledging the effectiveness of drama as a teaching tool, the impact it can have upon children's learning, the integral place of drama within language and literacy, and the social needs for theatre arts in education. The role of the drama coordinator (who may or may not also be the language coordinator) is to work with the staff to ensure that a comprehensive and successful drama programme operates from Year 1 through to Year 6. Responsibilities include the following:

- keeping well informed through journals, books and courses
- disseminating this information to staff
- running training for staff (e.g. INSET, working alongside them)
- inducting new staff into the school drama approach
- modelling good practice
- coordinating a comprehensive programme of theatre visits
- arranging visits by professionals to school
- coordinating seasonal events and maximising their potential for learning (e.g. Christmas performances)
- building up a collection of useful resources (e.g. plays, sound effects tapes, mood music)
- organising extra-curricular drama (e.g. trips, workshops, productions)
- organising theatre trips for staff and parents.

Certain inter-personal skills are also crucial! A flamboyant, confident drama teacher may inspire, but can also frighten other members of staff! It is important to be a good listener, and empathise with those who lack the confidence to teach drama. Encouraging them to try things in bite-size chunks is better than forcing them before they are ready.

Record keeping

Record keeping should be designed in ways which are useful, and if a whole-school approach to drama is adopted, this should include a whole-school approach to record keeping. This enables each teacher to build on the children's strengths. The competencies which were introduced in Chapter 10 have been set out in Appendix 4 as photocopiable record sheets which could be used as a starting point for your whole-school approach. Each of the five *Areas of Learning* appears on a separate sheet, with the Elements arranged in three columns. The competencies appear in each column, and can be highlighted or ticked when you think the child has achieved at that level. One set of these five sheets could accompany each child up through the school, and teachers would add to the same document, creating a cumulative individual record.

Theatre visits

The ideal expectation is that every child should experience live theatre every term. This would very likely include both trips out and visiting performers coming into school. The range of responses to the work of others which the National Curriculum requires cannot be built on one visit every two years. Children need to develop the 'theatre habit' and become confident critics. An annual visit for each class should be the absolute minimum.

Cost is only a problem if we allow it to become a problem! Many parents are delighted that schools will take their children to the theatre, and we should not assume that they will be unwilling to pay. We should, however, do our very best to ensure that parents understand the benefits of theatre visits, so that they appreciate the valuable learning rather than seeing it purely as leisure. However, not all parents are *able* to pay. An open pricing policy works in some schools (pay what you can afford). This clearly needs subsidy, and the size of that subsidy will depend very much on the economic catchment area of the school. Some approaches to funding subsidies are:

- use of ongoing PTA funds
- dedicated fundraising event once a year (e.g. The Theatre Fund Raffle)
- business sponsorship
- Arts Council funding
- Lottery funding.

It can also help some parents to offer a 'savings bank', where the children bring 50 pence each week. Appendix 4 includes a Theatre Visits Log which you might like to use as a record of the performances each child sees as they move through the school.

An introductory framework for planning drama in English

There now follows an introductory framework which offers suggestions for drama activities linking directly into the NLS range of fiction and non-fiction texts. Boxes have also been included in which you may like to note down topic themes in other curricular areas (e.g. The Victorians). Below this is a further box for additional drama activities on those themes. These have not been completed for you, because schools still vary enormously in their timing and approaches to the humanities and science. It is hoped that the ideas presented to you elsewhere in this book will enable you to plot in those drama activities where and when appropriate.

As with all the lists and frameworks in this book, the following planning suggestions are no more than that – suggestions! With this initial support, you can work with the rest of your colleagues to develop a planning framework for drama which will suit the needs of *your* school. Remember to work at a pace which is manageable and enjoyable. But don't hold back! Using drama with your pupils will bring you many rich rewards, and provide those children with learning opportunities which they will never forget.

DRAMA PLANNING FOR ENGLISH:YEAR 1

	TERM 1	TERM 2	TERM 3
NLS Range: fiction and poetry	Stories with familiar settings; stories and rhymes with predictable and repetitive patterns.	Traditional stories and rhymes; fairy stories; stories with familiar, predictable and patterned language from a range of cultures, including playground chants, action verses and rhymes; plays.	Stories about fantasy worlds, poems with patterned and predictable structures; a variety of poems on similar themes.
NLS Range: non-fiction	Signs, labels, captions, lists, instructions.	Information books, including non-chronological reports, simple dictionaries.	Information texts including recounts of observation, visits, events.
Drama Activity Starters	• office role-play area • writing lists in role as characters from stories • writing lists for teacher who is in role as forgetful character • teacher in role as story character to answer questions in the hot seat • whole-class improvisation following instructions on flip chart sheet (giant letter) journey through a magic forest • making labels for a character in a story, teacher in role	• library role-play area • miming fairy tale characters • improvisation changing endings of familiar stories • re-enacting stories with puppets as a play activity • changing the stories using puppets • re-enacting stories using masks	• travel agent role-play area • guided action through fantasy world • puppet actions to poems • puppet actions to children's own poems • dynamic duos, questioning about a visit (in role) prior to writing • re-enacting an event prior to writing

Other Themes This Term

Drama Activities

DRAMA PLANNING FOR ENGLISH: YEAR 2

	TERM 1	TERM 2	TERM 3
NLS Range: fiction and poetry	Stories and a variety of poems with familiar settings.	Traditional stories: stories and poems from other cultures; stories and poems with predictable and patterned language; poems by significant children's poets.	Extended stories: stories by significant children's authors; different stories by the same author; texts with language play.
NLS Range: non-fiction	Instructions.	i) dictionaries, glossaries, indexes and other alphabetically ordered texts ii) explanations.	Information books including non-chronological reports.
Drama Activity Starters	• pantomime role-play area • telling stories to mimed actions • improvisations and re-telling the event • writing instructions in role • detached voices giving instructions to mime • explore character motivation through hot seating	• tourist information role-play area • improvising endings from unfinished stories/comparing with actual ending • dynamic duos to explain a misdemeanour • dynamic duo interviews to discuss favourite story, poem or author • simulation of celebrations from other cultures	• school role-play area • research from non-fiction to create scenes/report live (non-chronologically) • create mini documentaries on area of interest (to encourage non-chronological approach) • teacher hot seating as expert in an area/children ask questions, teacher models non-chronological reporting

Other Themes This Term

Drama Activities

DRAMA PLANNING FOR ENGLISH: YEAR 3

	TERM 1	TERM 2	TERM 3
NLS Range: fiction and poetry	Stories with familiar settings; plays; poems based on observation and the senses; shape poems.	Myths, legends, fables, parables; traditional stories, stories with related themes; oral and performance poetry from different cultures.	Adventure and mystery stories; stories by the same author; humorous poetry, poetry that plays with language, word puzzles, puns, riddles.
NLS Range: non-fiction	i) Information books on topics of interest; ii) non-chronological reports; iii) thesauruses, dictionaries.	i) Instructions ii) dictionaries without illustrations, thesauruses.	i) Letters written for a range of purposes; to recount, explain, enquire, complain, congratulate, etc., ii) alphabetic texts, directories, encyclopaedias, indexes, etc.
Drama Activity Starters	• publishers' role-play area • dance drama on the senses • tableaux based on observations/link with follow up poetry or vice versa • Victorian schoolroom simulation, practising handwriting • in role planning a large building programme (brainstorming, leaflets, posters etc.)	• role-play area on historical theme • play reading • play blocking • reconstructed improvisations into play scripts/groups exchange scripts • writing stage directions • simulated events from other cultures	• 'science lab' role-play area (white coats, safe materials, forms, documents, reports, books etc.) • guided action through mysterious landscapes • guided imagery to explore strange environments • making mystery plays for the radio reading and writing letters in role

Topics This Term

Drama Activities

	TERM 1	TERM 2	TERM 3
NLS Range: fiction and poetry	Historical stories and short novels; play scripts; poems based on common themes, e.g. space, school, animals, families, feelings, viewpoints.	Stories/novels about imagined worlds; sci-fi, fantasy adventures; stories in series; classic and modern poetry, including poems from different cultures and times.	Stories/short novels that raise issues, e.g. bullying, bereavement, injustice; stories by same author; stories from other cultures. Range of poetry in different forms.
NLS Range: non-fiction	A range of text types from reports and articles in newspapers and magazines, etc.; instructions.	i) Information books on same or similar themes; ii) explanation.	i) Persuasive writing: adverts, circulars, flyers; ii) discussion texts: debates, editorials; iii) information books linked to other curricular areas.
Drama Activity Starters	• role-play area on theme from a story • improvisations on family issues • character documentaries • tableaux on feelings • tableaux on feelings with detached voices • newspaper stories: improvise story and parts not reported • interviews for magazines	• space station role-play area • performances of poems from other cultures • researching for tableaux • researching to create and present TV documentary • spontaneous improvisation in pairs on explanation • child in hot seat to explain (under attack!)	• role-play area with another cultural theme • tableaux on issues/bring alive the tableaux • paired improvisations on issues • poetry presentations with music and sound effects • designing adverts, circulars, flyers in role for specific purpose (e.g. new leisure centre) • simulated meeting to debate hot issue
Topics This Term			
Drama Activities			

DRAMA PLANNING FOR ENGLISH: YEAR 5

	TERM 1	TERM 2	TERM 3
NLS Range: fiction and poetry	i) Novels, stories and poems by significant children's writers; ii) play scripts; iii) concrete poetry.	i) Traditional stories, myths, legends and fables from a range of cultures; ii) longer classic poetry, including narrative poetry.	Novels, stories and poems from a variety of cultures and traditions; choral and performance poetry.
NLS Range: non-fiction	i) Recounting of events, activities, visits; observation records, news reports etc.; ii) instructional texts: rules, recipes, directions, etc. showing how things are done.	i) Non-chronological reports (i.e. to describe and classify); ii) explanations (processes, systems, operations etc.); iii) use content from other subjects.	i) Persuasive writing to put or argue a point of view: letters, commentaries, leaflets to persuade, criticise, protest, support, object, complain. ii) dictionaries, thesauruses, including I.T. sources.
Drama Activity Starters	• hotel kitchen role-play area • news programme with live reports and summaries • poetry as theme for improvisations • enacting plays from scripts • writing additional stage directions to play scripts	• role-play area on theme of myth or legend working with extracts from more advanced plays • longer exploration of narrative poem (e.g. Pied Piper, Ancient Mariner) • perform extracts from myths, others watch as if reporters on the scene, and make notes • puppet theatre of myths and legends	• office role-play area with I.C.T • performance of poetry with narrative action • writing letters in role following a relevant improvisation or simulation • exploring the use of masks in drama • telephone calls in dynamic duos to protest or criticise
Topics This Term			
Drama Activities			

DRAMA PLANNING FOR ENGLISH: YEAR 6

	TERM 1	TERM 2	TERM 3
NLS Range: fiction and poetry	Classic fiction, poetry and drama by long-established authors including, where appropriate, study of a Shakespeare play; adaptations of classics on film/TV.	Longer established stories and novels selected from more than one genre; e.g. mystery, humour, sci-fi, historical, fantasy worlds etc. to study and compare; range of poetic forms.	Comparison of work by significant children's author(s) and poets: a) work by same author b) different authors' treatment of same theme(s).
NLS Range: non-fiction	i) Autobiography and biography, diaries, journals, letters, anecdotes, records of observations, etc. which recount experience and events; ii) journalistic writing; iii) non-chronological reports.	i) Discussion texts; texts which set out a point of view; ii) formal writing: notices, public information documents.	i) Explanations linked to work from other subjects; ii) non-chronological reports linked to work from other subjects; iii) reference texts, range of dictionaries, thesauruses, including I.T. sources.
Drama Activity Starters	• TV studio role-play area • presentation of newsnight specials on a theme • re-telling of Macbeth with mime alongside puppet versions of Macbeth • contemporary improvisations of Macbeth characters	• futuristic role-play area • improvisations and simulations to provoke public debate • re-telling of The Tempest • puppet versions of The Tempest • interviews with Prospero and Miranda • writing in role • reading in role	• theatre role-play area with various costumes and props • hot seating characters and authors • re-telling of A Midsummer Night's Dream • mini performances of Pyramus and Thisbe • shortened version of A Midsummer Night's Dream
Topics This Term			
Drama Activities			

Useful Further Reading

Ackroyd, J. and Boulton, J. *Do Drama* (Books 1, 2 and 3). Northamptonshire County Council.
Excellent sample lessons for Key Stages 1 and 2 which provide a good supporting framework if you are just starting off with drama.

Clipson-Boyles, S.B. (1996) 'Teaching reading through drama', in: *Reading On! Developing Reading at Key Stage 2,* Reid, D. and Bentley, D. (eds.). Leamington Spa: Scholastic Ltd.
Practical ideas on how specific reading skills can be taught through drama.

Clipson-Boyles, S. B. (1998) 'Developing oracy through drama', in: *Frameworks for Talk,* Holderness and Lalljee (eds.). London: Cassell.
Approaches to planning oracy activities using drama, with case studies and examples.

Crinson, J. and Leak, L. (eds.) (1993) *Move Back the Desks*. Sheffield: NATE.
A very useful practical guide to drama ideas, underpinned by a recognition of the potential for language learning.

Heald, C. (1993) *Role Play and Drama*. Leamington Spa: Scholastic Ltd.
Particularly good for early years teachers. A practical resource book of ideas.

Heathcote, D. and Bolton, G. (1995) *Drama for Learning*. Portsmouth, USA: Heinemann.
A welcome revision of the seminal work, plus new ideas, from these two legendary proponents of the power of drama as a learning process.

Kay, M. and Cotterill, A. (1989) *Learning Through Action*. Wisbech: LDA.
An excellent book of approaches to teaching history and geography in particular through drama. Also gives guidance on the management of experiential drama.

Peter, M. (1994) *Drama For All*. London: David Fulton Publishers.
Developing drama in the curriculum with pupils with special educational needs.

Rankin, I. (1995) *Drama 5-14*. London: Hodder & Stoughton.
Useful lesson plans for drama across the primary age range.

Rawlins, G. and Rich, J. (1992) *Look, Listen and Trust: A Framework for Learning Through Drama*. Walton-on-Thames: Nelson.

Readman, G. and Lamont, G. (1994) *Drama: A Handbook for Primary Teachers*. London: BBC.
A book for drama with children from pre-school age through to Key Stage 3 which combines methodology with practicality.

Somers, J. (1994) *Drama in the Curriculum*. London: Cassell.
A sound theoretical base underpins this book which offers clear guidance on different components of drama teaching and theatricality.

Woolland, B. (1993) *The Teaching of Drama in the Primary School*. Harlow: Longman.
A practical guide to different methods of working in drama, from the use of poetry in small-scale improvisation through to performance and production.

Appendix 2

Useful Addresses

The Arts Council of England
Drama Department
14 Great Peter Street
LONDON
SW1P 3NQ
Tel: 0171 333 0100

Arts Council of Wales
Museum Place
CARDIFF
CF1 3NX
Tel: 01222 394711

Children's Theatre Association
Unicorn Theatre
6–7 Great Newport Street
LONDON
WC2H 7JB
Tel: 0181 543 4888

Community Dance and Mime Foundation
School of Arts
De Montfort University
Scraptoft Campus
Scraptoft
LEICESTER
LE7 9SU
Tel: 0116 2551551

The Drama Magazine
c / o Central School of Speech and Drama
Eton Avenue
LONDON
NW3 3HY
Tel: 0171 722 4730

Film Education
41-42 Berners Street
LONDON
W1P 3AA
Tel: 0171 976 2291

Learning Through Action Trust
Fair Cross
Stratfield Saye
READING
RG7 2BT
Tel: 01256 883500

National Council for Drama Training
5 Tavistock Place
LONDON
WC1H 9SS
Stamped addressed envelopes only please

National Drama
56 Empress Avenue
Wanstead
LONDON
E12 5EU
Tel: 0181 989 0997

The Puppet Centre Trust
Battersea Arts Centre
Lavender Hill
LONDON
SW11 5TN
Tel: 0171 228 5335

RSC Education
Royal Shakespeare Theatre
STRATFORD-UPON-AVON
Warwickshire CV37 6BB
Please write for information
The Scottish Arts Council
12 Manor Place
EDINBURGH
EH3 7DD
Tel: 0131 226 6051

Society for Storytelling
PO Box 2344
READING
RG6 7FG
Tel: 0118 9351381

2D Subscription (Teacher Packs)
AB Printers Limited
33 Cannock Street
LEICESTER
LE4 7HR
0116 276 9921

National Museum of Performing Arts
The Theatre Museum
1E Tavistock Street
Covent Garden
LONDON
WC2E 7PA
Tel: 0171 836 7891

Appendix 3

part two

Programmes of study: general provisions for all key stages

Drama activities should include

→ participation in as wide as possible a range of dramatic experience;

→ opportunities to learn how drama communicates meaning

→ opportunities to experiment with dramatic form

→ opportunities for pupils to make and perform plays as individuals and in groups

→ clearly differentiated tasks incorporating a variety of dramatic techniques and conventions, with access to appropriate resources

→ opportunities for self-evaluation so that pupils become able to recognise their levels of attainment in drama and use them as the basis for progression

→ opportunities to make connections between drama and other art forms

→ opportunities for pupils to incorporate in drama their skills, knowledge and understanding from other areas of the curriculum

→ exposure to a variety of live and recorded plays, including performances by their peers

→ the performance of plays in a variety of venues and for a variety of different audiences

→ opportunities to take part in devised and scripted performances

→ the use of all kinds of performance technology

→ opportunities for pupils to expand their dramatic vocabulary

→ opportunities to re-visit and build upon drama activities experienced earlier in the school

→ exposure to drama from different cultures and times

In order to illustrate the programmes of study in action, examples are given for each key stage in the pages that follow. In each lesson example, it should be possible to identify engagement in the three areas of experience – making, performing and responding.

Key stage 1 (5 to 7 years)

Programmes of study

Pupils should be taught to:

Explore ideas and stories through drama

Shape and communicate ideas and stories dramatically

Accept and engage in imaginary roles and situations

Perform to groups of peers

Respond to plays they have seen or been in

Pupils should be given opportunities to:

Engage in dramatic play

Explore the difference between pretence and reality

Discover the expressive possibilities of their voices and bodies

Perform in the classroom and in assembly

See plays performed by professional companies

Contribute their thoughts and feelings about a play to class discussions

Pupils be encouraged to:

Make decisions about the development of their work in drama

Relate what they have learned in drama to other areas of the curriculum

Explore the crafts associated with drama, such as masks and puppets

Express preferences about plays they see or take part in

See plays outside school hours

Examples

A class of six and seven year-olds has been working on the topic of 'Water'. The teacher tells the children a story in which a powerful queen plans to deprive a village of its water by diverting the river which flows through it to provide water for a new fountain in her palace.

Tables and chairs are pushed to one side and the pupils pretend to be villagers. The teacher then explains to the 'villagers' the queen's plans. When she has established the dramatic situation, the teacher asks the 'villagers' to prepare dramatic scenes to show the queen what might happen if the village loses its river. For example, some pupils, pretending to be gardeners attempting to save their parched flowers, devise a ceremony to make it rain.

To construct their scenes, the children use materials from the dressing-up box as well as classroom furniture. The 'villagers' perform their plays to the teacher 'in-role' as the queen.

A mime performer has been invited into a primary school that offers collaborative opportunities by linking regularly with a nearby special school. The pupils settle themselves on the 'story carpet' and the mime performer guides them in their imagination to a strange land where they participate in an adventure. The pupils learn how mime can be used to create an imaginary world.

Key stage 2 (7 to 11 years)

Programmes of study

Pupils should be taught to:

Improvise in groups with increasing competence and confidence
Use dramatic conventions
Use elementary lighting, sound, costumes and properties
Devise and perform plays
Use voice and body to communicate in a dramatic context
Analyse and evaluate performances
Identify different styles of drama

Pupils should be given opportunities to:

Explore and develop ideas in drama
Incorporate learning from across the curriculum in their plays
Use sound and lighting equipment
Take part in performances to peers and adults
See plays performed by professional theatre groups
Discuss, and relate to their own work, plays they see on television

Pupils should be encouraged to:

Relate the plays they make and perform in school to
activities out of school
Develop preferences and express opinions about plays
Develop an interest in theatre-going

Examples

A class of 10 year-olds has been reading, with the teacher, the novel, *Carrie's War*, by Nina Bawden, about wartime evacuees whose lives become entangled with those of the people amongst whom they have come to live. The story takes the child's perspective of adult behaviour and explores a child's experience of responsibility and guilt.

With their teacher working in role, the pupils play the parts of evacuees, using some of the situations from the book. Then, working in small groups, they create five minute scenes based on the general experience of evacuation which extend their understanding of some of the issues in the novel. The pupils have to decide on the setting and style of the scenes and solve any technical problems.

The completed scenes will be performed by each group to the rest of the class in a room with no specialist resources. The pupils in the audience will be asked to look for non-verbal clues in the performances which provide insights into the original story.

A class of eight year-olds visits a theatre to see a puppet company performing a comic play in which actors and puppets interact. After the production the actor/puppeteers explain how they combine performance and puppet manipulation. Back in school, the teacher helps groups of pupils devise short puppet plays for their peers, using some of the performance techniques they have observed.

End of key stage statements

By the end of key stage 1, pupils should be able to:

Making	*For example*
Explore the creative possibilities of extended dramatic play	Make a play using a popular story or myth
Organise their drama to communicate with others	Prepare a short play for assembly on the theme of 'friends and enemies'

Performing	
Participate as part of a group in dramatic make-believe for an audience	Enact, using simple costume and properties, what might happen when visitors from another planet arrive
Adopt and sustain a role or character in a piece of dramatic action	Play the part of Anansi in an improvised version of one of the African trickster tales

Responding	
Express their thoughts and feelings about drama they have been in or seen	Draw a picture of a favourite scene from a play
Talk about plays they have seen or in which they have taken part	Compare the professional marionette performance they have watched with the puppets they have made and used in class

End of key stage statements

By the end of key stage 2, building on attainment identified at key stage 1, pupils should be able to:

Making	*For example*
Participate creatively in the development of dramatic ideas	Use a variety of dramatic roles and situations to explore the idea of 'journeys'
Structure their drama to incorporate dramatic conventions and make effective use of space and other resources	Prepare a short play for Divali, using masks and mime acted in front of a simple backdrop

Performing	
Participate in the performance of a devised or scripted play	Act in a class performance of a play for parents about a Victorian Christmas
Enact different roles or characters in devised or scripted plays	Take the parts of several different characters in a play for assembly about the transportation of convicts to Australia

Responding	
Evaluate how well they and others perform against specific criteria and suggest ways of improving the work	Identify how a particularly dramatic scene was created in a performance of a new play by a young people's theatre company
Recognise the connections between their plays and a wider dramatic culture	Discuss the relationship between their play about the indigenous Americans and the Westerns they see on television

Theatre Visits Log

Name:

Play	Theatre	Date

At the theatre

My favourite characters

The scenery

My name is

My trip to the theatre...

NAME:

DATE:

On

I went to the theatre.

The play was called

It was about

My favourite character was

because

I didn;t like

because

The best part of the play was when

Theatre Review

by

The characters

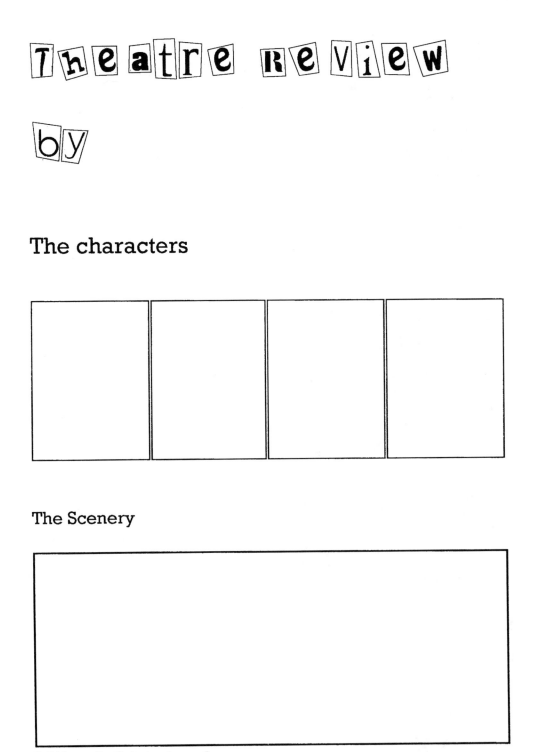

The Scenery

I liked this play because

Theatre Review

by

Review of

at

My first impression of this   play was

Particular good performances were given by

However,   as
was rather disappointing because

The set design was

One weakness of the production was

However, a real strength of this production was

Recommendation: out of 10

Telephone Messages

To:

From:

Time:

Message:

Telephone Messages

To:

From:

Time:

Message:

The Magic Ice Cream Cafe
MENU

DRAMA COMPETENCIES

1   Operational skills ...

name

PLANNING	PROBLEM SOLVING	WORKING COLLABORATIVELY
Can make independent decisions about tasks in the role play area.	Can break down a problem into component parts.	Can discuss and plan with a partner.
Can brainstorm ideas then sort into logical groupings.	Can speculate about the effects of a proposed solution.	Can offer ideas to a group of three or more.
Can plan at least three tasks in sequence to achieve an objective.	Can describe a problem from different perspectives.	Can change ideas after listening to others.
Can plan a presentation after initial stimulus from teacher.	Can offer a range of solutions which address different perspectives.	Can suggest appropriate roles to different group members.
Can plan a presentation using own ideas.	Can use reference materials to find information to solve a problem.	Can express disagreement constructively.
Can plan a short performance Including use of additional resources.	Can discriminate between different approaches to different types of problems.	Can address and help to resolve conflict constructively.

ADDITIONAL COMMENTS: Dates:

DRAMA COMPETENCIES

2   communication skills ...

name

SPOKEN LANGUAGE	WRITTEN LANGUAGE	PERFORMANCE SKILLS
Can express an idea or opinion in role.	Can use writing conventions in role for specific purposes.	Can perform action replays of characters in role play area for teacher.
Can change the mode of speaking for a change of character.	Can write brainstorming charts and sort into lists.	Can present mime and puppet representations to the class.
Can adopt a more formal tone in an appropriate role.	Can write in role from multiple perspectives.	Can represent different characterisations to rest of class.
Can communicate the ideas of a character clearly to an audience.	Can write in a range of genres for multiple imagined audiences.	Can project voice to larger audience (e.g. in assembly).
Can use Standard English appropriately in role.	Can write instructions, narratives and scripts for presentations and performance.	Can present appropriate voice and movement of characters to a larger audience.
Can express opinions using supporting evidence in Standard English and other forms.	Can write in direct speech, indirect speech and script form.	Can explore different approaches to voice, gesture and emotion of characters.

ADDITIONAL COMMENTS: Dates:

DRAMA COMPETENCIES

3   creative skills ...

name

USE OF IMAGINATION	USE OF RESOURCES	INTERPRETATION
Can introduce ideas from stories into role play.	Can select costumes and props appropriate to role during plays.	Can recreate a story in role play area.
Can organise ideas into a short mime or puppet show.	Can discuss character feature when designing puppets and masks.	Can transfer learning between drama and other subjects.
Can invent alternative endings to stories and plays.	Can use appropriate resources for sound effects.	Can interpret dialogue and stage directions from a play script.
Can organise own ideas into a short play on a given theme.	Can decide on appropriate props, costumes and sound effects to enhance performance.	Can discuss themes in plays performed by professionals.
Can bring different ideas to a given theme.	Can select and use different recorded music to create atmosphere.	Can transfer style elements from professional theatre into their own drama.
Can develop ways of communicating ideas in a theme of their choice.	Can plan, make, and evaluate own use of resources, including basic lighting.	Can make links between approaches to presentation and themes.

ADDITIONAL COMMENTS: Dates:

DRAMA COMPETENCIES

4   understanding ...

name

CHARACTER	AUDIENCE	CONTENT
Can talk about a character played in role.	Can extend role play to show the teacher.	Can discuss the sequence of events after role play.
Can discuss the difference between real and imagined characters.	Present confidently to the class.	Can use prior learning in the drama.
Understands that people can have different perspectives on the same event.	Presents confidently to a larger audience.	Can research information for the drama.
Can express an opinion which is different to their own.	Considers the aural needs of the audience.	Can identify further research needs after the drama.
Can explore movement and voice of characters.	Considers the visual perspectives of the audience.	Can present key facts in dramatic form.
Can explore character motivation within situations.	Understands that individuals in an audience will respond differently.	Can interpret key facts from different perspectives.

ADDITIONAL COMMENTS: Dates:

DRAMA COMPETENCIES

5   responding ...

name

LISTENING	ANALYSING	EVALUATING
Listens to a partner in role and responds appropriately.	Justifies reasons for choices and decisions in a play.	Discuss at least two things they like about a piece, and why.
Watches the work of others and remembers key points.	Discusses feelings and thoughts about particular characters.	Can support discussions of things they don't like with ideas for improvement.
Can discuss different ideas or issues which have been presented in a drama.	Can discuss how they felt as a particular character.	Compare two pieces on the same theme.
Asks appropriate questions arising from what has been heard.	Can predict how a different character might have felt.	Evaluate their own work against the teacher's expectations.
Can distinguish between different types of speech including Standard English.	Can compare how two different characters might have felt about the same event.	Can compare their work with previous pieces.
Recalls things heard in a previous occasion to use in discussion.	Discuss reasons for the style of presentation by professionals.	Can identify alternative approaches which might have been better.

ADDITIONAL COMMENTS: Dates:

References

Arts Council of Great Britain (1992) *Drama in Schools*. London: Arts Council of Great Britain.

Berk, L.E. (1994) 'Why children talk to themselves'. Scientific American.

Bolton, G. (1979) *Towards a Theory of Drama in Education*. Harlow: Longman.

Brecht, B. (1966) *The Caucasian Chalk Circle*. London: Penguin. (First published in Berlin in 1953).

Browne, A. (1983) *Gorilla*. London: Julia MacRae.

Browne, A. (1992) *Zoo*. London: Julia MacRae.

Bruner, J. (1986) *Actual Minds, Possible Worlds*. Cambridge, Massachusetts: Harvard University Press.

Burnett, F. Hodgson (1994) *The Secret Garden*. London: Penguin.

Burningham, J. (1978) *Would You Rather....* London: Random House Children's Books.

Clay, M. (1979) *The Early Detection of Reading Difficulties*. London: Heinemann.

Clipson-Boyles, S.B. (1996) 'Teaching Reading Through Drama', in: *Reading On! Developing Reading at Key Stage 2*. Reid, D. and Bentley, D. (eds.). Leamington Spa: Scholastic.

Clipson-Boyles, S.B. (1996) *Supporting Language and Literacy*. London: David Fulton Publishers.

Clipson-Boyles, S.B. (1997) 'Drama'. in: *Implementing the Primary Curriculum. A Teacher's Guide*. London: Falmer Press.

Collier (1996) 'The Education of Language Minority Students: United States Policies, Practices and Assessment of Academic Achievement', in: *Teaching and Learning English as an Additional Language – a new perspective*. London: SCAA.

DES (1975) *A Language for Life (The Bullock Report)*. London: HMSO.

DES (1988) *English from 5 to 16 (The Cox Report)*. London: HMSO.

DES (1988) *Report of the Committee of Inquiry into the Teaching of English Language (The Kingman Report)*. London: HMSO.

DFE (1995) *National Curriculum Requirements for English*. London : HMSO.

DfEE (1998a) *The National Literacy Strategy: Framework for Teaching*. London: HMSO.

DfEE (1998) *The National Literacy Strategy: Literacy Training Pack*. London: HMSO.

Edwards, V. (1995) *Speaking and Listening in Multilingual Classrooms*. Reading and Language Information Centre: Reading University.

Frank, L. (1992) 'Writing to be read: young writers' ability to demonstrate audience awareness when evaluated by their teachers'. USA: *Research in Teaching English*, Vol. 26.

Goodman, Y. (1990) 'The Development of Initial Literacy', in: *Knowledge About Language and the Curriculum*, R. Carter (ed.). London: Hodder and Stoughton.

Heald, C. (1993) *Role Play and Drama*. Leamington Spa: Scholastic.

Heathcote, D. and Bolton, G. (1995) *Drama for Learning: Dorothy Heathcote's Mantle of the Expert Approach to Education*. Portsmouth, USA: Heinemann.

H.M.I. (1990) *The Teaching and Learning of Drama*. London: HMSO.

Hutchins, P. (1970) *Rosie's Walk*. London: Picture Puffins.

Hughes, T. (1993) *The Iron Woman*. London: Faber and Faber.

Kallie, J.V. (1991) *Structured Informality. English for Speakers of Other Languages 5–16*. Oxfordshire County Council Commercial Services.

Kane, M.B. and Khattri, N. (1995) *Assessment Reform: a work in progress*. USA: Phi Delta Kappan, 77(1).

Kay, J. (1994) 'Duncan Gets Expelled', in: *Two's Company*. London: Penguin.

NCC (1991) *Drama in the National Curriculum* (poster). London: HMSO.

OFSTED (1996) *Annual report of Her Majesty's Chief Inspector of Schools*. London: HMSO.

Raison, G. (for the Education Department, Western Australia) (1994) *Writing. Developmental Continuum*. Melbourne: Longman.

Readman, G. and Lamont, G. (1994) *Drama. A Handbook for Primary Teachers*. London: BBC.

Rossi, R.J. and Stringfield, S.C. (1995) *What We Must Do For Students Placed at Risk*. Phi Delta Kappan, 77(1): USA.

Sainsbury, M. (1996) *Tracking Significant Achievement in Primary English*. London: Hodder and Stoughton.

Slavin, R.E. et al. (1996) *Success for All: Roots and Wings*. Baltimore, Maryland: Johns Hopkins University.

Somers, J. (1994) *Drama in the Curriculum*. London: Cassell.

Stanovich, K. (1980) *Towards an Interactive Compensatory Model of Differences in the Development of Reading Fluency. Reading Research* 16, 32–71.

Vygotsky, L.S. (1978) *Mind in Society*. Cole et al. Cambridge, Massachusetts: Harvard University Press.

Wagner, B.J. (1979) *Dorothy Heathcote – Drama as a Learning Medium*. Hutchinson Books.

Way, B. (1967) *Development Through Drama*. Harlow: Longman.

Wells, G. (1986) *The Meaning Makers*. London: Hodder and Stoughton.